5 EASY STEPS

TO GET OUT OF DEBT

This book is dedicated to my friends and family who believed in me and inspired me

INTRDUCTION

Welcome to the "5 Easy Steps to Get out of Debt!" This book has been structured to get you out of debt fast! The "Foundation Series" is a fast-paced program which allows you to take immediate action and start seeing results. The "Advanced Strategies" includes information, motivation, and strategies that build off the previous. Have fun and enjoy life while getting out of debt!

ABOUT THE AUTHORS

David and Sheila is a married couple with two children who currently live in Washington State. David is a Paramedic and has been working in the medical field for ten years. Sheila is a Nurse and has been working in the medical field for four years. The couple were born and raised in Washington State and lived ordinary lives. After reaching a period of financial hardship which put strain on their relationship, they knew it was time to make a change. They created a lifestyle which brought more happiness into their life, lived their lives to the fullest, and reached their financial goals!

COPYRIGHT

TABLE OF CONTENTS

Foundation Series

P.R.I.D.E

This five-step program is organized using the acronym P.R.I.D.E

P: Prepare your mindset

R: Reorganize your life

I: Identify your goals

D: Determine your plan

E: Execute

Taking P.R.I.D.E in yourself means you value yourself and those around you. The steps you take in the P.R.I.D.E method will lead you to your goals and reinforce this statement. Financial problems have a way of taking away from those important in your life. They lead to stress, anger, depression, and eventually overall poor health. They prevent you from experiencing the life you always dreamed of.

Each step in this program will prepare you mentally and physically, until you are ready to begin eliminating your debt.

We will go through each step in detail as we get into the program. Let's dig in!

Step 1: Prepare Your Mindset

Your mindset is the most important factor in eliminating your debt! Your thoughts have shaped your life and created the situations you are in today. It is essential to change the way you think in order to change your future.

Changing your mindset will not come overnight. It requires constant attention and persistence. Changing your mindset is nothing more than changing a habit. It takes around 28 days for your mind and body to adapt to change. So for the next 28 days, I want you to apply the principles in these lessons to everyday life. Once you master the techniques, you will find an overall improvement in the quality of your life!

Your subconscious mind is composed of the thoughts and experiences from your past in which great emotion was involved. These thoughts help guide our future actions. For the majority of people, deep rooted negative thoughts prevent them from taking action. The fear they experience stops them from taking risks. Instead they stay in their "comfort zone." There is never any gain or achievement.

In changing your mindset, we will conquer the fears that have been implanted in our subconscious. We will use the power of positive thinking, mixed with positive emotion, to attract positive events in our lives. We will reduce stressors in our lives so we can focus on our goals. And, we will steer clear of any negative thoughts, emotions, or situations that drain our energy.

In order to make change, you will need to get out of your comfort zone. Take a moment and think about how this will really feel. Getting out of your comfort zone means you will be going against the grain of society who tend to "play it safe." You may feel nervous, anxious, and may have an overwhelming feeling of doubt. Your mind will keep searching for escape routes as an excuse to leave this uncomfortable environment. As your mindset changes, and as you begin to see the benefits of your actions, you will establish a new level of comfort.

Every thought we create in our mind has a reaction in the world around us. The world responds to the energy our mind puts out. When we stay focused on something we don't want in our lives, or we focus on the things that are going wrong in our lives, we are only drawing more of what we are focusing on into our lives.

Negative people attract negativity into their lives and they cannot figure out why they have had such poor luck. They focus on the problem instead of focusing on what they really want in life.

Negative thoughts create stress and the body's reaction to stress leads to long-term health problems. Accumulated stress caused from financial problems has been linked to chronic hypertension, or high blood pressure, which can place you at a much greater risk for heart attack or stroke. Long term stress also results in headaches, tightness in the chest, insomnia or difficulty sleeping, feelings of anger, anxiety, and depression. Not to mention the added strain it places on relationships with those close to you.

The best way to relieve stress is to take a break from whatever is causing it. You may need to move to a quiet environment where you can be uninterrupted for a few minutes. Take some deep, controlled breaths and clear your mind. Focus on your goals instead of focusing on your problems. I prefer to spend time away from my problems at the gym. I find I can really clear my mind and re-focus my energy through a stimulating workout. Remember the harmful effects stress has on your body. Reducing stress will improve the quality of your life!

Another helpful exercise is to make a list of your appreciations. Find a quiet area, take out a blank piece of paper, and write down a list of the people, things, and experiences in your life you are thankful for. Begin each with, "I am grateful for..." and explain what you are grateful for and why. Review this list daily so you can stay focused on the things that make your life enjoyable.

You are in control of your future, and the control is right there in your head. It is your mind and thoughts. For now on, eliminate any negative thoughts that may enter your head. When a negative thought comes in, tell yourself that you will not accept it and let it go. Replace it with a positive thought. The dominant thoughts in your head should lead you toward your final goal.

If you tell yourself, "I will never get out of debt, this is impossible!" then you will never get out of debt. Replace that thought with something like, "Getting out of debt may be a challenge, but I know I will succeed," and believe it!

Your success will depend on how much faith you have in yourself. You must eliminate any doubt from your mind. Doubt causes you to second guess your decisions and prevents you from taking action. You may need to work on boosting your self-confidence. Take a piece of paper and write down all of your positive qualities and successes. There is no timeframe in which the successes occurred, just write them all down. Mentally go back in time to when these successes occurred and remember how you felt. How has this shaped you to where you are today? How can this help you in your future goals of financial freedom?

Another powerful exercise is to picture yourself where you want to be at the end of this program. Close your eyes and imagine yourself already in possession of your final goal. Imagine how it would make you feel to have accomplished such an outstanding goal. Imagine how it would positively impact you and your family's lives. Believe in yourself that these goals will be achieved!

In the advanced strategies section, we will provide more depth to the power of the mindset. This program is designed to rapidly move you through the foundation of the Debt Rescue program so you can begin to take action today!

Step 2: Reorganize Your Life

The organization phase is divided into three parts:

- Income
- Monthly Expenses
- Spending

In the advanced strategies section, we will focus on a fourth category: Life. Organizing your life is one of the most important tasks in accomplishing long-term success. In this program, our goal is to get you started taking immediate action.

Organization is necessary to gain a full perspective of your situation. Debt results from a problem in one of these three categories. We need to bring the problem areas out front and center so we can begin to take care them.

We will begin by taking a look at your income. This is the money you and your partner are bringing in on a regular basis. Your income will provide the funds necessary to achieve your financial goals.

Next, we will take a look at your monthly bills. We will establish when the bill is due, how much is owed, and what the remaining balance is.

For now the goal is to organize the information to a single place. Later, we will begin to explore any areas of opportunity to reduce spending and build a Debt Pay-Down fund.

Finally, we will assess your spending habits. We will begin by organizing your monthly spending into categories, determining if the expense was essential or non-essential. Later, you will determine which non-essential spending habits can be eliminated to help move you toward your goals faster.

Income Organization

Let's take a look at how much money you bring in on a regular basis. This will allow you to get a realistic assessment in order to develop your financial goals. Add all of your income sources to the "Income Organization" worksheet. This worksheet is available to download for free at SAHDLife.com/DebtForms.

Obtain copies of the last two months pay stubs for anyone in your house who will contribute to your goals. Many companies mail statements to your address. You may also obtain copies online or by contacting your employer.

Take your total income after taxes, or "Net Pay," and average them per month.

If you get paid every two weeks you may take the total of the last four pay stubs and divide it by two to get your monthly average.

If you want to get more technical, take the total of the last four pay stubs and divide it by four to get your average pay per paycheck. Take the average and divide it by two. This gives you an average per week. Now, take that number and multiply it by 52, the number of weeks in a year. Finally, divide this total by 12 months to get a more accurate monthly average.

Log the results on your "Income Organization" worksheet under average monthly income. Write in your current month's actual income and future, or expected, income. Provide a monthly total at the bottom. Utilize this worksheet each month to show your expected income

Organize Those Bills

It's time to take that big pile of bills off your desk and organize them! You will need to obtain information about all the monthly bills you expect next month. You may need to search through old bank statements or checkbook stubs to locate them all.

Once you have all of the bills for the month gathered, we will use the "Bills Organization" worksheet to sort them out. This worksheet is available to download for free at SAHDLife.com/DebtForms.

Begin by writing your bills in the space provided, and organize in descending order by due date. You will need to know when the bill is due, how much the minimum payment is, if there is a grace period and when, and the total balance owed. Knowing the A.P.R is informative, but will not come into play in this program. You will learn the details behind this strategy in the advanced strategies section.

You may need to perform some research to get all of the information needed to complete this worksheet. Please be patient with this step. It will pay off large in the end!

The P.R.I.D.E number will be explained in detail later on in this lesson, but for now we can tell you it is a tool used to prioritize the bills that needs to be paid off first.

The "Bills Organization" worksheet is the same tool I used to eliminate my debt and achieve my dreams! I included two columns that kept me organized and allowed me to keep track of my payments more efficiently. When you send a check in the mail, or are waiting for a pending online payment to process, mark the box labeled "Money Sent." When you confirm the payment has been received, mark the box labeled "Bill Paid." This helps avoid the mistake of assuming a bill has been paid because the check was sent when it hasn't cleared your account yet.

I always wrote down the confirmation number from payments I made. This proved to be beneficial a few times when there was a dispute about a payment received. Having the confirmation number allowed me to prove my case.

Take your time and fill out the form completely. At the bottom, add your total monthly minimum payments in the box labeled "Total Monthly Debt" and add the total outstanding debt in the box labeled "Total Balance Owed." This may be tough to look at right now, but the step is incredibly important to your success.

Only one more organizational step left. Let's keep moving forward!

Organize My Spending

It's time for the last step in the organization stage of this program. We need to take a peek at what you have been spending. This step can be scary. At Debt Rescue, we don't focus on negative events from the past.

We are taking a look at what was spent so you can identify the problem areas and make a positive adjustment in the future.

Developing the proper mindset also focuses on your thoughts when it comes to consumerism. For many, spending money on "things" creates a sensation of fun and excitement. Eventually, the burden of debt sets in when it comes time to pay the bill. Life is all about indulgence, but until your finances are under control it should be in moderation. We will differentiate between indulgences and rewards, which can bring positive changes to your mindset and attract success, in the advanced strategies section. For now, we want you to weigh the positives and negatives of specific purchases.

Begin by getting a copy of your last two months bank statements. You can obtain these by logging on to your bank's website or by visiting your local branch and requesting copies. If you are a cash spender, you may need to estimate expenses right now. In the future, collect receipts from all of your purchases and log your expenses for the next month.

Use our free "Spending Organization" worksheet to organize your spending for the month. You may download this worksheet for free at SAHDLife.com/DebtForms.

Categories are provided to the left for organization of major spending items. In the "Monthly Tally" column, you will log each expense as either "Essential" or "Non-Essential."

Essential spending includes anything required for you to live and make money. This may include food, water, and shelter. It may also include the vehicle you use to get to work, the gas needed to operate your vehicle, clothing, and personal hygiene. What you decide to label as "Essential" is completely up to you.

Non-essential spending includes any items purchased that do not fit into your definition of "Essential." Just because an item is labeled as "Non-Essential" does not mean you can no longer spend money on it. If your weekly enjoyment includes spending dinner at a restaurant with good friends and family, then do so. If you can find other areas of opportunity to cut expenses, while still fulfilling your goals, there is no problem.

We will work on reducing the amount you spend on non-essential purchases later in this program. For now we will focus on organizing your spending into categories and labeling each either "Essential" or "Non-Essential."

Go through your statements or receipts and begin tallying each expense. Determine the item's category and then mark the item as either "E" for essential or "N" for non-essential. Keep track of the money spent on each item, because you will add up the total cost of each category at the end.

After you have tallied all of your expenses for the month, and added up the costs of each category, provide the total of all categories in the box labeled "Total Monthly Spending." Then, take the entire worksheet and add up the individual "E's" and "N's" tallied. Provide the totals in the boxes provided at the bottom of the worksheet.

Take a look at the results of this worksheet. You can immediately find areas in your current spending where you may have the opportunity to save money.

After you complete the "Spending Organization" worksheet, you will need to complete the "Financial Balance Worksheet" to determine your "Debt Pay-Down Money." The Financial Balance Worksheet can be downloaded for free at SAHDLife.com/DebtForms.

Your "Debt Pay-Down Money" is the money you will use to accelerate your progress in completing your goals. It consists of the money remaining from your income after you deduct monthly debt and spending expenses. It is the funds available to make additional payments toward your debt. We will go over "Debt Pay-Down Money" in more detail when we discuss debt-elimination strategies.

All three documents: Income Organization, Bills Organization, and Spending Organization worksheets should be updated on a monthly basis. Staying organized and completely aware of your financial situation will place you in a much better position to be successful.

Step 3: Identify Your Goals

Now it is time to lay out your future! We will establish immediate, short-term, long-term, and final goals.

Goals are essential to the success of a plan. You need to have a destination in mind, or an overall purpose, when establishing your plans. If you don't know exactly where you're headed, it will be difficult to get there. This is why we begin with goals.

We are going to start at the end. First, we will create your final goal. Your final goal is established to provide an overall purpose. If your overall purpose is to become financially free, then you will develop plans that lead you to this outcome. Do not cut yourself short here. The possibilities are endless!

Why do you want to change your financial situation? In what ways would it benefit you and those close to you? These questions are the starting point for developing your goals. To begin, we will establish your "Why."

Your "Why" is the reason you want to achieve your final goal. You may want to achieve financial freedom so you can spend more time with your children or so you can finally quit your job and pursue a career in a field you really enjoy. You may want the freedom to start your own business or some other investment. No matter what your "Why" is, it will be the prime motivator that will get you to your final goal.

My "Why" was simple: My wife and I were both working full time and we were barely making ends meet. We had a mortgage, two brand new car payments, a credit card, and tons of medical bills. Our spending was out of control and our debt had piled up. The stress had placed a major strain on our relationship. I had told my wife, "I don't care if we lose the house and the cars; I just want us to be happy." My "Why" was for my family. Find that powerful motivation when developing your "Why."

Take a blank piece of paper and write down your reasons for wanting to achieve your final goal. Keep this as a reminder of why you started to take on the challenge of accomplishing your dreams in the first place and to provide motivation when the going gets tough.

Now that you know where you're going, and have established your "Why", you need to establish goals that lead you there. Your immediate goal is in place for instant gratification. It should be a goal which is easy to achieve and promotes taking action. Simply, setting your immediate goal as completing this educational program and beginning your plans at once is sufficient. The successful completion of goals creates positivity in your life and builds your self-confidence.

After your immediate goal has been established, you will develop a short-term goal. This goal will typically range from three to six months to complete. The short-term goal will provide a path toward the completion of your long-term and final goal.

Imagine where you would like to see your financial situation in the next three to six months. Develop a short-term goal and write it down on the "Financial Goals and Plan Worksheet." This worksheet will be provided at the end of this lesson after all of the concepts of this lesson have been presented.

After completing the short-term goal, you will need to develop five sub-goals that lead you to the completion of this single goal. What steps will be necessary to take now, or in the upcoming weeks to achieve this goal? Using the "Sub-Goals" section of the "Financial Goals and Plan Worksheet," write down five milestones that will need to be reached to complete your short-term goal.

Your long-term goals are in place to provide long-term guidance in carrying out your plans. These will keep you on track to achieving your final goal.

To establish your long-term goal, imagine where you would like your financial situation to be in one to three years from now. Develop a long-term goal and write it down on the "Financial Goals and Plan Worksheet."

After completing the long-term goal, you will need to develop five sub-goals that lead you to the completion of this single goal. What steps will be necessary to take after the completion of your short-term goal in order to accomplish this goal? Using the "Sub-Goals" section of the Financial Goals Worksheet, write down five milestones that will need to be reached to complete your long-term goal.

Your goals do not have to all be about money. Be sure and set aside time each month to spend time with the people who are important in your life. Spending time with good, positive people will help you gain a support system, boost confidence in your abilities, and improve the quality of your life by reducing stress.

There must be a reward for accomplishing your goals. You should include a reward after each primary goal is achieved. You want your positive actions to be awarded. This not only gives you motivation to accomplish your goals and makes you feel better about your accomplishment, but it also implants positive memories into your subconscious mind that promotes similar behavior in the future. As you continue working through your plans, your subconscious will pull out positive, enjoyable memories to keep you motivated and on track!

Your rewards must be paid for in cash prior to earning the reward and must not set you back from your goals. Remember, this program is all about enjoying life while paying off debt. If you devoted all of your time and resources towards eliminating debt, what would the quality of your life be? The time saved may not be worth it in the end. Reward yourself and enjoy your life now!

Rapidly eliminating your debt and achieving your financial goals will not come without making changes in your present ways. You will need to make some sacrifices along the way. It will feel uncomfortable at first, but the end result will make it all worth it. Remember, successful people do what unsuccessful people are too uncomfortable to attempt. The end result is your final goal. The question is: What are you willing to sacrifice now in order to achieve that goal?

On the ambulance, I must weigh the risks and benefits of giving any certain medication. Before I choose to administer, I must determine if the medication will be more beneficial or more harmful to my patient. You can do the same with your purchases. First decide if the purchase was essential or non-essential. Then, weigh the positives and negatives of each non-essential purchase and decide for yourself. If you find the purchase would be more harmful to your goals, then do not spend money on it in the future.

An alternative to living without a certain product is to replace it with a cheaper option. Most American's spend around $5.^{00} at the coffee stand each day. That adds up to $150.^{00} a month! The alternative would be to make the same coffee at home. I used micro-ground coffee packets and flavored syrup to make a delicious iced latte each morning for about $1.^{25} a drink! I can still enjoy a tasty coffee each morning, and enjoy a monthly savings of $112.^{50}.

Figure out which spending categories you can eliminate and where you can find cost-effective alternatives. Come up with a plan that will keep you excited throughout the process. If you lack excitement and determination, your plan has already failed. In order to be successful, you will need to enjoy life while carrying out your plans.

Small gains can go a long ways in this program. Remember, pennies turn into dollars and your dollars pay down debt.

Increasing your monthly income is not the only way to get out of debt. A more reasonable approach is to reduce the amount of monthly expenses. Be creative when you search for ways to decrease your debt and spending. Think outside of the box. With enough determination and positive thinking, the answers will come to you. They are there; you just have to find them!

- Find ways to increase your monthly income
- Find ways to decrease your monthly debt
- Find ways to decrease your monthly spending

Using the methods you determined above, fill out the "Financial Goals and Plan Worksheet." You can download our "Financial Goals and Plan Worksheet" for free at SAHDLife.com/DebtForms.

Return to the "Financial Balance Worksheet" to update your "Debt Pay-Down Money" balance. Note the difference!

In the advanced strategies section, we will explore many conventional and unconventional methods used boost your progress.

You will need to be as specific as possible when determining your goals. Establish an exact deadline that is realistic and obtainable, and know exactly how much money you will need to accomplish each goal. Your mind can only bring you what you ask for. In order to do this you will need to be precise.

Your goals should be displayed on your fridge or another public location within your home. Go over the goals you have established each time you pass by them, and before going to bed at night. Spend time in a quiet area and read your goals out loud. Close your eyes and imagine yourself already having accomplished your goal. Now, feel the emotions you would experience after its accomplishment. Hold these thoughts and images in your mind for as long as possible. The universe works in mysterious ways. As long as you stay determined on achieving your goal, the universe will deliver! Believe that the end-result of your goal is out there waiting for you to receive it. There should be absolutely no doubt in your mind that you will accomplish your goals. If you are feeling embarrassed or doubtful about the goals you established, then you have not proven to yourself your faith in them. As part of your mindset change, you need to have confidence in yourself and have an undoubting believe that your goals are obtainable. Changing your mindset is absolutely necessary when it comes to eliminating debt and becoming financially free!

Step 4: Determine Your Plan

Now that you have a clear picture of your goals, you are ready to start paving the path from where you are today to where you want to be. Your plans will become the roadmap toward achieving your final goal.

Someone once asked me, "How do you eat an elephant?" The answer is one bite at a time! We will use this concept to knock out your debt. If you stand back and look at the entire problem, it can appear to be larger than you can handle. But, when you develop a plan and take out a single problem at a time, the situation becomes manageable.

We will introduce you to a proven strategy that takes your debt and breaks it down into manageable pieces. Our system seeks out the bills with the highest potential to accelerate your progress and begins taking them out one by one. It utilizes techniques to maximize efficiency and produce rapid results.

This system functions using the P.R.I.D.E number. The P.R.I.D.E number looks at three factors of a bill to maximize your debt pay-down potential: the total outstanding balance, number of payments remaining, and the minimum monthly payment.

Without proper training, many people make small additional payments toward the principle balance on multiple accounts each month. Others have been instructed to pay off the debt with the highest interest rate first. Neither strategy maximizes efficiency or produces the most rapid results.

The Debt Rescue strategy produces quick and easy results using a calculated method! You will need to have a copy of your Monthly "Bills Organizer" worksheet. Earlier in the program, we organized your bills by due date. We are now going to re-organize your monthly bills by your P.R.I.D.E number.

In order to get your P.R.I.D.E number, you will need to divide the total remaining balance by the minimum monthly payment. Write the resulting number in the P.R.I.D.E number box.

Once you have completed this exercise for all applicable bills, you will want to re-organize your monthly bills organization worksheet. Use a blank "Bills Organization" worksheet and re-organize the bills by their P.R.I.D.E number from lowest to highest. As you begin re-organizing, you will notice that the bills that are easiest to pay off with the highest minimum payments appear at the top of your list.

You have now established a list of the top priority bills you will begin eliminating. The bill with the lowest P.R.I.D.E number will be targeted first. The strategy continues on in ascending order by P.R.I.D.E number until all of your debt is gone.

This strategy maximizes efficiency and produces rapid success by focusing all of your resources toward paying off the bill that will contribute large amounts to your Debt Pay-Down Money balance in the shortest amount of time.

Your Debt Pay-Down Money is the money that remains after spending and minimum monthly payments have been deducted from your income. This money is used to pay down a single debt each month: the debt with the lowest P.R.I.D.E number. The more money that can be placed in this fund, the sooner you will see results.

As soon as the debt with the lowest P.R.I.D.E number is completely paid off, you will take its minimum monthly payment amount and add it to your "Debt Pay-Down Money" balance. Take this opportunity to congratulate yourself for making progress, and update your "Financial Balance Worksheet."

The next step is to start paying off the debt with the next lowest P.R.I.D.E number with the higher balance in the "Debt Pay-Down Money" fund.

The strategy can be better understood through a visual example. In the "Advanced Debt Elimination Strategy" example, we will walk you through a sample scenario.

The scenario includes a family who has a mortgage, two car payments, student loan, credit card, and a personal loan. Their debt totals over $183,000! We show you how the application of this method allows them to pay off their debt in a little over 8 years! This includes their home!

Each step is explained in detail. This document can be downloaded for free at SAHDLife.com/DebtForms.

As you go through this example scenario, notice that the family did not take any action in reducing their debt or spending. Just imagine the results that could have been obtained with a more aggressive strategy.

In addition to your debt-elimination strategy, you will need to develop specific plans to carry out your immediate, short-term and long-term goals, and their sub-goals. For each one developed, you will create a detailed plan of action in order to achieve that goal. Write out a plan for each goal on the "Financial Goals and Plan" worksheet.

As I am preparing myself for the day on the ambulance, I typically run myself through a "Mental Scenario" of certain calls I could come across. As I run through the scenario, I proceed through the routine steps of running the call, anticipate any problems ahead, obtain the necessary knowledge, prepare a pre-plan for the possible event, and determine if the outcome would have resulted in success or failure. When necessary, I obtain the knowledge required to create a positive outcome and keep running through the mental scenario until I have reached success.

This strategy aids in creating plans to pay off your debt as well. Running your plans through mental scenarios will help mitigate risk and give you the confidence necessary to take action.

If you reach a point where fear is preventing you from taking further action, you may need to run your problem through the "Worst Case

Scenario" worksheet. This worksheet allows you to gain a full perspective of the situation by exploring it from all angles. It is a visual representation of the mental process I must complete when managing emergency scenes.

On emergency scenes, first responders do not have all of the tools available to determine the exact nature of a problem. Sometimes we rely on subtle clues and our intuition to determine the severity of a situation. Based off symptoms described, the patient's presentation, and the objective information we can obtain, such as vital signs, we must make a decision on treatment. We consider treatment decisions based on the potential problem. We must consider the worst-case scenario and take all necessary steps to avoid such scenario from developing. With all of our knowledge and skill, we perform interventions to direct the potential outcome towards the best-case scenario.

I have developed a "Worst-Case Scenario" chart that can be downloaded for free at SAHDLife.com/DebtForms. This chart will relieve stress and anxiety of impending situations by allowing you to weigh the risks and benefits before pursuing certain actions.

Your plans will be the blueprint for your upcoming journey. They will provide the framework to help guide your decisions as you work towards your goals. They should be flexible enough to adapt to any unforeseen changes in life that may occur. You will need to continuously monitor your progress and re-evaluate your plans. Ensure they are still leading you toward your goals and within the specific timeframe. Your plans are flexible, but your goals are not.

Make any necessary changes to your plans along the way and continue making progress until the completion of your goal.

I would like to congratulate you on staying committed with this program and being persistent toward achieving your goals! There is only one more thing left to do: Take Action!

Step 5: Execute

The time has finally come to take action. There is no turning back now. There is no option for retreat!

Take the goals you have created, and the plans you have developed, and begin at once. The hardest part of getting started is taking that first step. Conquer your fears and take that leap of faith. Do not wait until you feel completely ready. Do not hold off until you have all the knowledge necessary to achieve your goals. Have faith in yourself and know that the world will deliver exactly what it is that you desire. Focus on your goals and take action immediately. There will never be a *perfect* time to begin. The best time is right now!

Do not let anyone or anything get in the way of your final goal. Keep your focus and your energy around the positive people in your life. Maintain confidence in yourself and faith in your plans. Prove the naysayers wrong with your results!

Remember the concepts taught in this program and review them often to maintain proficiency. A high emphasis has been placed on mindset in this program. Review the material until you feel you have comprehended the meaning. In the right mindset, any obstacle will be seen for what it really is: just another step on the road to success.

The sooner you come to the realization that life will not play through perfectly, the easier your life will become. You will meet failure. How you respond to it will make all of the difference.

When you come across a barrier in your plans, the best thing to do is to remain calm. Stand back from the situation, take a deep breath and draw in oxygen to your lungs and brain. This will help relax your mind and allow it to think creatively. Gather as much information about the problem as possible. Try not to hold too much emotional attachment to the problem and do not focus on any potential money lost. Your job now is to solve the problem, recover from the loss, reorganize yourself and continue making progress on your goals. No matter how bad the problem may feel now, it will be nothing compared to the benefit of you achieving your final goal.

Throughout life, failure has been given a negative condemnation. In Debt Rescue, we need to learn the new definition of failure. We look at "Failure" as a stepping stone to your future success. Many great minds in history have failed their way to success. You must expect to do the same.

Look at each "Failure" as a lesson learned that will lead you closer toward your goal. Each perceived failure brings with it acquired knowledge, experience, and eventually confidence. Learn from your failures, never quit, and you will reach your goals! "Quitting," or giving up when you reach failure, is the only true definition of "Failure." Remember, winners never quit and quitters never win.

At Debt Rescue, we want you to have fun and enjoy life. Getting out of debt is not about becoming rich. It is about having the time and resources to live life the way you want and to spend quality time with people important to you. Get ready to live life's journey in ways you never imagined possible! A whole new world of opportunities is about to open itself up to you!

Advanced Strategies

Welcome to the Advanced Strategies section of "5 Easy Steps to Get out of Debt!" By now you have gained the Foundation Knowledge required to rapidly start your progress and begin achieving your goals. We will now introduce some more advanced concepts and strategies so you can really accelerate your progress.

Approach this section with an open mind. The more strategies you implement, the faster your results, and the sooner you will have the freedom and resources to live life the way you want!

Get ready for a life changing experience!

Prepare Your Mindset

Mindset and Why is it Important?

Your mindset consists of the dominant thoughts that occupy your brain. These thoughts affect your perception of life, your mood, your health, and your future success. Your mindset is who you were, who you are now, and a reflection on what you will become.

Your subconscious mind is composed of thoughts and experiences that have shaped your life until today and help guide how you react to a situation. Your thoughts enter the subconscious only when great emotion was involved. This explains why some people hold unreasonable fears such as a phobia.

Growing up, I had a phobia of throwing up. I would do anything in my power to stop from retching when I was sick. Just the sight of someone else becoming ill would bring nausea to my stomach. I was told many stories about amusement park rides making people sick. That was enough to keep me away.

Over time, I finally conquered my fears. I work as a Paramedic, so I am around disgusting fluids all the time and they don't bother me. I finally rode my first roller coaster in high school and it was one of the most amazing experiences. Today, I still love the thrill of freefalling and going upside down. Even thought I had consciously conquered my fear, I still noticed a response in my body every time I would step in line for a ride.

I began feeling a tremor in my arms and legs. A sick feeling would come over me and I would lose my appetite. I had no conscious fear of the roller coaster, but deep inside my brain, the subconscious would take over.

Our goal in this program is to re-program your subconscious mind when it comes to your happiness, your health, and your financial success.

You can change your mindset. Maintaining positive thoughts about your outlook on life has the power to change your mood, your health and your future. Look for the positives out of every situation. No matter how bad the situation may appear, keep a positive mindset.

Negative thoughts create disease in our bodies. The stress caused by the overwhelming flood of negative thoughts in the mind eventually leads to physical damage internally.

Stress triggers a natural protector in the body. This protector is called the 'Fight or Flight' response. As with anything in life, too much or too little may be harmful.

The 'Fight or Flight' system responds to fear, stress, and perceived threats. It works by dumping the hormone Epinephrine into your blood stream, which prepare the body to either retreat from a threat or face it head on.

In the days of survival, the system worked as a protector that made the difference between life and death. In current, civilized times, the response has a tendency to become activated too often because of the added stress we place on our lives.

Epinephrine increases your blood pressure by tightening up your blood vessels and increasing your heart rate. Those with a negative mindset and constant stress experience frequent release of this hormone throughout their lives. Over a long period of time, the result is organ damage and possible life-threatening conditions. Increased blood pressure places you at risk for heart attack, stroke, and kidney failure.

The toll of stress also affects your mental and emotional health. Increased levels of stress have been linked to depression, anxiety, and difficulty sleeping.

There is hope for your future. Maintaining a positive mindset will improve your mood and place you in greater health. Your future is dependent on a change in your current mindset. Without a change in your thoughts, you could not expect a change from your current circumstances.

Before you get any further into your debt-elimination strategies, you need to make positive changes in yourself. Find out what it is that causes added stress in your life and work to change or eliminate it.

In order to achieve your hopes and dreams, you need to have a clear, stress-free mind. In the 'Foundation Series' of the Debt Rescue program we organized your finances. Use the same concept and organize your life. Simplify your life as much as possible as you continue to work towards your goals.

Constant conditioning of the mind is necessary for change to occur. Only allow positive thoughts to enter. When a negative one finds its way in, get rid of it immediately and replace it with a thought from a more positive perspective.

Do not focus on the problems in life. Instead focus on what you are grateful for and the resources you have available to help you achieve your dreams. Instead of thinking, "This will never work," ask, "How can I make this work?"

A change in mindset will not only make you feel better inside, but it will also shape your future. A future that once appeared hopeless will begin to shed light. Change starts with you. And it starts with just a single thought.

Your Thoughts Are Real Things

Your thoughts have shaped your life to where you are today. These thoughts affect your perception on life, your mood, and your health, and your future success.

The universe has a natural way of drawing particular objects, people, or situations into your life. The power driving this natural phenomenon is in your thoughts.

The most powerful, dominant thoughts you hold in your head, backed by emotion and faith, will determine your future. You are drawing in the physical manifestation of these thoughts into your life.

This power has been explained through science and religion. No matter what your beliefs in the origin of this power, understand that it is real and always in action.

The advantage is that you have control over your own thoughts. No one else can control them. No one else can change them. They are yours, and when used properly they will provide a substantial amount of prosperity in your life.

Utilizing your mindset for success begins with regulating the thoughts that enter your brain. Your thoughts should be positive, reinforcing thoughts that boost your self-esteem and spread love and joy to others.

When a negative thought enters your mind, immediately dismiss it and replace it with a positive one. When searching for a positive thought, think of what it is in that moment that you are thankful for. If you are driving to work and got cut off by another driver, do not yell and scream at the driver and hold hateful thoughts in your head for the remainder of the trip. Instead, think of what you are grateful for. You may be grateful for having avoided an accident and remained safe. You may be grateful for having a reliable mode of transportation and a job that pays the bills. Focus on these positive thoughts, and let the other driver pass.

The universe responds to the primary thoughts that occupy your mind, but it doesn't differentiate between what you want and what you don't want. It only listens to the focus of the thought. If the focus of your thought is "I don't want to fail," then you will attract more failure in your future. It is important to keep all negative thoughts outside of your mind, including those which focus on what you are trying to avoid in your life.

If you fill your mind with thoughts such as, "I want to get out of debt," you will be drawing in more debt to your life because that is the center of your thoughts. Your primary thoughts need to be directed towards your final goal. If your dream is to live financially free, then that is where your thoughts will need to center. If you fear failure, focus on succeeding.

The universe responds to those thoughts with great emotion and conviction. You need to have faith that the universe will deliver whatever it is you ask for. A powerful exercise is to close your eyes and imagine yourself already in possession of your final goal.

Visualize yourself living without debt. Imagine where you would live? What would you do for a career now that money was not an issue?

Experience the emotions that would be felt by achieving that goal. Feel how happy you would be the moment you finally accomplished your dreams. Experience how this would benefit your life and your family.

Believe in your dreams. Imagine yourself already in possession of your final goal, today.

In the "Foundation Series" of the program, you developed goals and placed them in a public location within your house. Each time you pass by these goals, repeat this exercise. See it, feel it, and believe it!

Look at those around you. Unfortunately, the world is predominantly negative. People look for the bad qualities in any situation. They find the negative aspects to complain about and make this their center of focus. This is seen in reviews for businesses, social media posts, and everyday conversations with those around us.

Finding a predominantly positive person can be rare these days. In this program, we will cover many circumstances when going against the grain of society will be more beneficial to your success. Understand that negative people may try and bring you down. If you keep doing what everyone else is doing, you will achieve the same results they have. If you are not satisfied with those results, it is time to make a change. Begin by surrounding yourself with a positive support structure.

We will stay honest and ethic as we carry out our plans to achieving success. We will not alter our morals for our own benefit. We will not change who we are. We will only bring out more of the good we already have and share it with the world.

This program is about getting out of debt. We also promised a life-changing experience. We will encourage you to enjoy life while achieving your dreams, and inspire you to live your life to the fullest, starting today. We want you to make the most out of the relationships with those close to you. We want your positive characteristics to shine through which will inspire others to like you, trust you, and follow your lead to success.

Why Your Old Mindset Led You to Failure

Your environment is a product of your thoughts and feelings. Growing up, we were taught various ideas from our peers. Persuasive ideas from others have shaped your mind to where it is today.

Many people who were raised poor end up living poor as adults. Those raised in a middle-class environment end up in the middle-class. They were taught a lifestyle, and naturally they imitated it when it was time to live on their own. They do what they see others do and they got the same results.

We have all been taught methods for managing our finances. You may have been told, "Old cars will cost more to maintain than a new car" or, "You have to buy on credit, there is no other way to afford large purchases." All of the persuasive ideas have shaped your mindset to where it is today and has led you to your current situation.

Take a look at where the advice is coming from. You want your financial advice to come from a role model, or someone you wish to emulate.

People who are struggling financially remain in the situations they are in because they fall in the trap of emulating the majority. They get out of school and get a credit card because they are told this is the way to build your credit. They get an education and rack up student loan debt. They are told it will be easier to pay off the loans once they are making the big bucks at their new job. They eventually meet that special someone and begin making a family. They are encouraged to buy a brand new car because old cars are unsafe, unreliable and will cost more in maintenance. Then, they go and buy a house, and before they know it all they can afford each month are the minimum payments on their debts with just a bit of extra "fun money" left over.

I fell into this same trap. I was told, "This is the way life is," and I saw that everyone else lived the same way. It felt normal. That is, until I came across a major turning point in my life.

My wife and I had brand new cars and had just purchased a house. We had student loan and credit card debt, but the payments were comfortable. After had our first child, the medical bills from the hospital and prenatal visits had maxed out our budget. We had no cushion room and on many instances needed to borrow money or charge purchases to keep our heads above water. This problem was not going to go away anytime soon. It was at this point that we had realized we were in trouble.

We had reached our breaking point, and we were finally ready to take on this problem we had created. I was willing to lose it all before I was going to live paycheck to paycheck for the rest of my life.

I hope you do not have to reach your breaking point to find the motivation to change. We were in trouble well before we realized it. We did not know because our influences in life told us that we were living normal. The debt we accumulated was actually looked at as an accomplishment.

We are not here to place blame. We are here to shape our future. Many of the ideas from the past were beneficial for their times. We are living in different times, now. Different times require a different way of thinking and acting.

I wanted the time and freedom to live my life and experience the growth of my children. I did not want to be trapped in a job with no options. I did not want limitations in life that debt had caused my family. I strived for change and found that the change had to come from within. It had to start with a change in my thoughts.

I began taking on my situation with faith that I would succeed. I had no doubt in my mind that I would reach my goals. I knew the road ahead was going to be tough, and I was prepared for the challenge. I allowed no retreat as I marched forward and began taking out one issue at a time until I had reached my goals. It felt like a huge weight had been lifted off my shoulders!

We want nothing less than for you to find happiness in your life and achieve your dreams! With a change in mindset, anything you aim for will become a reality. Continue working on changing your mindset and focusing your dominant thoughts on your final goal.

You will need to surround yourself with a positive support structure. Find a financial role model in your life. Also, find a positive personality in your life. You want to spend as much time with those people who inspire you to succeed and want to see you achieve your dreams. They will provide a powerful, positive influence to your spirit.

Communication with Your Friends and Family

Communication is a major part of any relationship. This point may have been overstated over the years, but it is still relevant. In order to ensure your success, we will need to go over some essential factors when it comes to communication.

As you proceed on your journey and begin achieving your financial goals, you need to stay in communication with those close to you. Spending time developing financial goals and plans has a way of taking away from those who care about you.

You will want to keep your close friends and family informed. Tell them you are starting to take control of your finances and are striving to improve your situation. Share with them your final goal and let them know how you achieving your goals will benefit them. Ensure that you will make time for them in your busy schedule.

As people make major changes in themselves or their situations, they may be looked at as being selfish or non-conforming to society. With proper communication, you can set the record straight before any judgmental thoughts have a chance of being passed around.

Explain to your close friends and family why you are changing your financial situation. Back in the "Foundation Series" you developed your "Why." Use the major points from your "Why" to enlighten them.

My wife and I imagined a life where we had the freedom and resources to take our friends and family on a small "Get-Away" every holiday season. We would have the ability to fund the trip; all they would need to do is show up. We imagined a world where we could spend more time with our children. We desired to have the ability to take care of our parents at home in a warm, comfortable environment when they were older. The true benefit of getting out of debt was to build experiences with those we loved and to enrich their loves, along with our own.

Make sure you are taking time to keep in touch with your friends and family as you continue through this program. Set aside time each week, or each day, and let them know you are still there. You can call, send a text message, post on their social site, or see them in person. Do not unintentionally cut these people from your life. If you do not spend the same quality time with them during this program as you did prior, you will probably not have contact with them after you achieve your goals. You may have successfully accomplished your financial goals, but you will find yourself lonely and unhappy.

Money is not everything. Maintaining a relationship with those close to you will bring out the joy and happiness in your life you are seeking.

Make your promises and deliver them. Actions speak louder than words. Build trust in the early stages by keeping your word. Your friends and family may fear change will alter you so much they won't recognize you anymore. Ensure them that this is not true, and gain their trust by following through on your promises. In the end, you will be a happier person with more time and resources to really experience life to the fullest and spend it with those you enjoy spending time with.

When spending time with your close friends or family, do not only speak about your finances. You will push most of them away faster than if you had avoided them in the first place. Use good judgment and determine if your recipient takes interest in your new expedition, first. In the beginning, you may find it hard to hold people's interest when speaking about your visions. Remember, actions speak louder than words. Once you show them results, they will start asking you questions.

Discrepancies in opinions between partners can be a major hurdle to conquer. An important initial step is to establish a final goal that both you and your partner can agree on. Speak openly about any difference in opinion and compromise on goals and strategies until you can find common ground.

You and your partner should work together to accomplish the tasks in this program. One person making the sole decisions will not guarantee cooperation from the other. If your partner does not have the motivation to sit down and go through the steps, then simply include them in the decision-making through your conversations. Ask them what they want in life and why. Incorporate these responses into your plans. Both you and your partner should feel that you have an equal share in the decisions that are being made.

What if your partner is not on board? In the development of your successful mindset you have learned two key points:

- There is no obstacle that is impossible to conquer once you have achieved the proper mindset
- You can have anything you put your mind to

There are no excuses in this program. Everybody has a unique situation and not everyone may proceed through this program with the same ease.

Share your thoughts and dreams with your partner and inspire them. You may also get started yourself and motivate them through your actions. A good leader does so by example, not through force. Begin fixing your portion of the spending and monthly bills. Do not affect your partner's lifestyle, but do include them in your goals. Allow them to benefit from your efforts.

Another quality of leadership is the willingness to do more work than you are being compensated for. You must be willing to take sacrifices for the better of the entire team.

Maintain a positive relationship. Do not let the stress of money get in the way of what is free in this world: love and friendship. Even if you had nothing, in a true relationship you will still have each other. Cherish this and maintain a positive mindset as you move on through the program.

Leadership

You are in control of your future. In order to make a difference in your current situation, you will need to take charge. Leadership will play an important role in your upcoming ventures.

You, and your partner, are responsible for all of the decisions that need to be made. You are also responsible for the outcome of those decisions. In this lesson, I will teach you the characteristics of a good leader. Begin to apply these traits to your daily life. The traits of effective leadership will guide your thoughts and future actions in the right direction.

Leadership requires self-confidence. You will gain confidence in yourself through actions which result in a positive outcome. This starts by stepping out of your comfort zone and taking action. To mitigate the risks, you should seek an education, motivation from a role-model, and draw upon past experiences with a positive outcome.

You have already started receiving your financial education in this program. Your financial education does not stop here. You should always be in pursuit of gaining knowledge and experience throughout life. In every situation you encounter, ask questions and get clarification on issues from the experts in that field. The higher you can build your financial IQ, the easier it will be to improve your financial situation.

Find a financial coach, or a mentor, in your life. Is there anyone you know, or can get in contact with, that has already been through your situation? Do you know anybody who is currently in a situation where you would like to see yourself? Find a person in your life that will provide the inspiration and motivation to keep you making progress towards your goals. When the going gets tough, they will be the ones who push you to succeed because they believe in you.

As you develop a successful mindset, you should have no problem drawing upon positive memories from your past. Do not dwell on something from the past that did not go well or caused you to lose money. This will only lower your confidence and draw in more failure in your future through negative thoughts. Know that you will not make the same mistake again because you learn from it.

This program was developed to help boost your self confidence as you progress through the steps. We start with accomplishing small victories to give you the encouragement to keep making progress toward your larger goals.

With increased confidence, you will be able to make faster decisions and take action without the fear of failure. You will have the assurance that the right decision was made and will not have the urge to quickly change your mind.

Leaders make quick decisions, take immediate action, and change their minds slowly after acquiring additional knowledge. The world is happening all around you. When it's time to make a critical decision, the world does not pause for you to make up your mind. You will need to be able to pull the trigger before an opportunity passes by or a situation gets worse.

The best thing you can do is make the right decision. The next best thing you can do is make the wrong decision. The worst thing you can do is make no decision at all. Indecision, or the inability to reach a decision, will be more costly than making a bad call.

A leader is not afraid to take action. Maintain the faith that you will reach your final goal and understand that there will be some obstacles to conquer along the way.

On the ambulance, the condition of our patients can change rapidly. Quick, confident decisions are necessary to achieve a positive outcome.

For example, as a Paramedic, I get a patient who was involved in a vehicle accident and needs a specialty trauma surgeon. The patient appears to be between 14 and 18 years old, but we have no identification. I know my pediatric trauma center will allow patients up to age 16; otherwise they need to go to the adult hospital.

If I don't make a quick decision, the patient's condition could deteriorate. If I choose the wrong hospital, they may not be fully capable to treat the patient. What do I do?

I make a decision! I stick with the decision until I have overwhelming evidence that can further guide the path I have already taken. At that point, I can re-evaluate and decide if I want to change my mind or stick through the original plan.

It doesn't matter if I chose the pediatric trauma center or the adult hospital. Either decision was better than sitting on scene and trying to gather the complete story before taking action. To reach the best decision possible, we rely on the facts presented at the time, our knowledge, and our intuition.

In your financial situation, don't be afraid to take action. You don't need to know every detail of how your goal will be reached before making that first step. Just aim for the goal, have faith in your abilities, and the rest will fall into place naturally.

It takes courage to make change happen. A good leader does not view mistake as a failure. They learn from their mistake and continue on toward a positive change.

Leadership requires problem solving. If you find yourself searching for the answer to a problem, but only drawing a blank mind, this is most likely a problem of over-thinking. This does not reflect your ability to come up with a quick, creative plan to solve the problem.

A rush of ideas reaches the brain all at once and your mind attempts to sort them all out. Take a step back from the situation, relax, and allow your mind to do its job. Most people become anxious as this occurs, which only makes the problem worse. Do not focus on the problem. Find a solution and the problem will go away.

Leadership requires self-control. In order to achieve self-control, you should write out plans for your finances and your life. Follow these plans and reward yourself for completing your goals.

Practice controlling your indulgences. You know where you want your plans to take you and you know if certain purchases will allow you to accomplish your goal or hinder your progress.

Your mind should constantly be focused on your final goal. As you wake up, on your drive to work, during your lunch break, on the drive home, and as you lay in bed at night, you should be maintaining positive thoughts and reinforcing faith in your plans. With a properly developed mindset, self-control will come naturally.

When you find a product or experience you desire, write it down and hold onto all of your ideas in a single location; your "Wants List." These can serve as rewards for accomplishing your goals. They are also excellent sources for building a vision board.

A "Vision Board" is a picture-based poster board that displays all of your dreams and achievements you wish to accomplish. It reinforces the mind to work towards their acquisition and draws in the power of the universe to turn that into reality.

Make a Vision Board and post it in your room or office. To make a vision board, take blank poster board and paste images which represent your dreams and desires. In the center of the board, create a blank space to write a passage beginning with, "I am grateful for..." and describe the images on your vision board in present tense. Describe these items as if they were already in your possession. Finish the passage by describing how it will benefit you, your friends and family.

Take a few moments each day and visualize yourself already in possession of each item on the board. Imagine yourself already in that exotic destination you dream of visiting. Read the passage in the middle of the board. See it, feel it, believe it, and it will become reality.

Leaders are particular about details. The attention you pay to details when gaining knowledge, gathering information about your situation, and drafting plans will determine your outcome.

The saying goes, "If it is predictable, it is preventable." Critically think your way through your strategies to determine their strengths and weaknesses. This is best accomplished through the "Mental Scenario." The details you miss now may result in problems for you in the future.

Do not get so caught up in the analysis phase that you do not take any action. Procrastination will not produce results. Your decisions will be based on facts, your knowledge, and your intuition. Gather as much detail as necessary to make an informed decision and take action immediately.

Leaders are fearless, or at least it appears that way. The truth is they experience the same fear everyone else does. The difference is they keep moving forward in the face of fear. They have confidence in themselves and their team. They have faith they will reach success.

Fear, alone, is what stops most people from taking action. This emotional response stems from the subconscious mind in an attempt to protect you from the unknown. Your mind can be your worst enemy. This is why it is so important to develop the successful mindset that has the faith and determination to push past fear and reach success.

Successful people do what unsuccessful people are too uncomfortable to attempt. It feels uncomfortable to move forward past your fears. You will feel anxious and may become unsure about yourself. This is an opportunity to make a huge impact on your subconscious mind and really develop your mindset. The subconscious mind holds deep within those memories and thoughts which had great emotion attached. The emotion of fear, in addition to a successful outcome, will program your subconscious to no longer fear the unknown but to embrace the opportunity. Push past your fears, take action, and find success no matter what.

Run through your "Worst-Case Scenario" worksheet when faced with a situation that creates fear. This will ensure you take the correct path in making decisions.

Leadership is not natural. It is an acquired ability which requires persistence in practicing the skill through practical application. Constantly work on fine-tuning the attributes of a leader and apply them in your personal life. Eventually the skills will feel natural and happen without thinking.

Do not focus on whether you will be criticized for your decisions. They are your choice and there is a reason you made that decision. Know how to back up every decision you make by understanding how it will benefit you and those around you in the long run.

Effective leadership happens through being the prime example and motivating others. Leaders never use force or intimidation to get results. That style is ineffective and only creates resentment toward the intimidator. An effective leader will have gained the respect from their team. Gain the cooperation of others by getting them to like you and trust you. Inspire them to follow your direction as you lead by example. You cannot demand respect, you must earn it.

Achieve the Proper Mindset

Your thoughts are the drawing board for your future. Changing your thoughts today will shape your tomorrow. Once you achieve the proper mindset, a whole new world of opportunity will open itself up to you.

In order to maintain a path of success, you will need to change the way you think about your finances.

Your Mindset When It Comes To Income:

When asked how to get out of debt, most people respond by increasing their income. They pull overtime shifts or pick up a second job with the hope of paying off their debt. As this method may be effective, it is not the most efficient. It will steal all of your time and allows for no creativity.

You do not want to work harder to achieve your goals. Make life easier on yourself. My wife and I were able to pay off a majority of our debt while both working part-time because we changed other aspects of our situation.

Plan to lower your monthly debt and reduce your spending. When you hold onto more of the money you already earned, you will be able to make large advances without working harder to achieve it.

I always thought back to how my financial situation was when I was 18. I was living on my own, but I split rent at an apartment with two other roommates. I did not have a vehicle payment because I drove a used car. I only made $8 an hour, but I was able to do more with that measly pay rate at a 20-hour work week that I was making paychecks 6 times that.

When I made more money, I also spent more money and had larger debts. When planning to improve your financial situation, try to get yourself as close to the financial situation you were in when you were 18, but keep the higher pay rate.

Your Mindset When It Comes To Expenses:

Your expenses include every dollar you spend beyond your monthly bills. In the "Foundation Series," you categorized your spending as either "Essential" or "Non-Essential." For now, we will focus on your mindset when it comes to the non-essential purchases.

Just because a purchase is labeled non-essential does not mean it is not allowed in this program. If that were true, you would be leading yourself into one miserable experience. You will have to take control of your desires in order to make progress toward your financial goals.

My wife and I rewarded our progress by planning family vacations after achieving major progress toward our goals. Amongst many day trips, we flew to Hawaii for a week to attend a family member's wedding, spent 10 days in Belize for a romantic getaway, and drove to Leavenworth with the family for Christmas each year. We were able to afford these excursions because of the priorities we placed on our spending. And, we were still able to accomplish our goals, either on time or sooner than planned.

Finding areas to reward ourselves was important to our progress because it kept us motivated to continue achieving more goals. The feelings of success and accomplishment the reward brought helped program positive experiences into our subconscious mind that would make success even easier.

When it comes to spending, keep those items and experiences that will enrich your life and bring happiness. Anything that may cause stress or resentment toward the purchase later will not allow you to achieve your goals and should be avoided.

Do not sacrifice other's enjoyment for your own gain. If you family celebrates holidays by exchanging presents, plan for this event and participate. By giving, you will create more happiness and love in your life. This is the key to acquiring your final goal.

Even though we kept a tight budget, our friends and family still received presents from us on their birthdays, at Christmas time, at their baby shower, during their wedding, and even on Grandparent's day. Those who give freely without selfishness will receive greater amounts in the future.

If you want to get ahead financially, you need to get rid of the idea of "Keeping up with the Joneses." They are living paycheck to paycheck and do not know how they are going to pay off all of their debt. Comfortable amenities do not create comfortable living with the burden of debt constantly lingering over.

For the next couple years, if you are willing to live like no one else is willing to, you will have what everyone else would only dream of.

Your Mindset When It Comes To Debt:

Most people look at their debt as something that can't be changed until the debt is paid in full. We will take a closer look at various types of debt soon. Just remember, when it comes to your monthly bills, everything is negotiable and anything can be changed.

There will be some bills that you do not absolutely need but may provide entertainment, such as a subscription to a magazine or online video rental site. There may be some bills that take up valuable money, but provide you with physical and mental benefits, such as a gym membership. There may also be bills that are essential to your daily living, with the appearance that nothing can be done to change it, such as car payments and insurance.

You need to get creative when it comes to your monthly debt. We will get into great detail about this topic later, but for now we will provide a simple analogy. Live like you were living 10 years ago. Take every bill you have and change it in some fashion. What were you driving 10 years ago? What kind of phone did you have? Did you have a roommate who split the cost of rent? Using this analogy, how could you change your current situation to better reflect that from your younger self?

Your Mindset When It Comes To Credit:

Credit is the concept of using other people's money to make large purchases before one can actually afford the item. Most people could not conceive a life without using credit. How would you buy a car? How could you possibly afford a house?

There is only one side that benefits from the use of credit, and that is the banks. A social standard has been created that using credit to purchase the things in life that you desire is completely acceptable and absolutely necessary. This system will only put you in debt and keep you in debt for a long time.

As you pay off debt, do not plan on purchasing with credit ever again, unless the purchase will make you more money than the cost of borrowing. This is an advanced concept and will be taught in a future financial program that answers the question, "What do I do now that I'm out of debt?" For now, you will find that as you pay off debt and change your mindset, you free up more than enough money, whether physical cash or intellectual currency, to fund major purchases without using the banks.

Intellectual currency is the money that can be created or saved by creatively thinking your way through problems or situations. We will cover this concept in detail later in this program.

Stay persistent, make some personal sacrifices, and reward yourself as you make progress. Before you know it, you will be living beyond your dreams.

Reorganize Your Life

Organizing Your Life

In the "Foundation Series," you organized your income, expenses and debt. You filled out four worksheets through the process which helped you gain an overall perspective of your financial situation.

There is one more important detail we will discuss before we continue making progress. All of your effort could come to a halt if you do not address this one issue. You need to organize your life.

It would have been impossible for me to accomplish the goals I had if my life was not in order. You need to ensure your life at home, work, with friends, and family is organized and content before you can begin making actual progress on your finances. As you work through the program and begin accomplishing your goals, it is easy to lose sight of these areas in your life. This is why we address this issue early in the program.

It may feel that you do not have enough time for everybody in your life while you are working towards your goals, but with proper organization and planning it will be obtainable.

Begin by categorizing the people important in your life. You will develop a plan to focus your time on each category of people later in this program.

Categories may include your partner or spouse, your best friend or your group of friends, your family or in-laws, and your children. Whoever is important in your life where you want to ensure a long and happy relationship, make a category for them.

Plan time to spend with these people each month to ensure you are maintaining a positive relationship and bringing more enjoyment and happiness.

Use a blank calendar to organize your life. You could use any calendar, but we included a template for your convenience that you may download for free at SAHDLife.com/DebtForms.

Begin filling out the calendar with you and your family's current schedule. Place your work schedule, and that of your partner. If you have children, write in their scheduled events, too.

This will give you a clear picture of you and your family's obligations and free time. The open days on your calendar are your areas of opportunity to schedule events with family and friends.

This calendar will be brought back later in the program when you develop life goals and establish plans for spending time with the loved ones in your life.

Life is too short to be wasted. You have an opportunity to live life to the fullest today. Before you know it, your opportunities will pass by. Maintain relationships with those you care about. They are going to be the ones you continue to experience life with! Proper planning will ensure you have the opportunity to live your life to the fullest and enjoy time with friends and family while completing your financial goals.

Right now, you are taking on a huge load of responsibility. You will be balancing home life and work life with your friends and family; all while achieving a more secure financial future. You will be expected to accomplish all of this with limited time and resources. The most difficult time in your life is going to be now. It will get easier from here on out. As you make progress toward your goals, you will begin to free up more time and resources. Life will get easier, I promise!

Many people depend on your success. Keep them in mind and remember your "Why" as you organize your life.

Determine What You Want and What You Need

In the medical field, we rely on a system of triaging patients, or organizing them by the severity of their illness or injuries, to determine who needs to treated first. On a scene with multiple patients, we first look for those with life-threatening injuries and classify them as a high priority. Next, we look for those with major injuries which are not life-threatening and classify them as a medium priority. Last, we classify the remaining patients with minor injuries as low-priority.

You can do the same with your spending and your debt. Using a classification system, you will need to determine which monthly bills or spending items are causing the most financial bleeding.

Use your "Monthly Bills Organizer" worksheet and your last month's bank statement, or any other document showing your monthly spending, and begin to prioritize these expenses.

Label each item on a scale from 1 to 10 to indicate its priority in your current financial situation. One is a low priority item which has very little importance to you and could be eliminated easily. A ten will signify that the item is of major importance and cannot be taken away.

Organize the priority of your purchases and tallies using our "Spending Priority" worksheet. This document can be downloaded for free at SAHDLife.com/DebtForms.

Using this worksheet, add up the total spending in each priority level to gain a picture of how much money is going out and how important those items are to you, according to your newly developed goals and current financial situation.

When you take your focus off the emotional attachment to the purchase, and simply focus on a number, the decision will come much easier to reduce or eliminate it. Keep your mind on the achievement of your final goal, and you will find you don't miss the low priority items.

Managing Your Habits and Hobbies

Habits and hobbies cost us a lot of money, and unfortunately many businesses have made major profits on the habit forming products they sold. Simply stopping cold turkey, no matter the habit, may not be easy to do, either physically or mentally.

Completely stopping any habit or hobby will take dedication. You must be strong mentally to take on the challenge. There are a few factors to consider when deciding whether or not to quit.

Habits and hobbies, alike, form similar mental and physical changes in our bodies which cause us to resist quitting.

Your body adapts to the neurochemicals that are released while enjoying a habit. The neurochemical, Dopamine, is released into the bloodstream and gives your body a sensation of pleasure and satisfaction. With repetition of the habit, your body begins to adapt to this high level of Dopamine and your mind associates the feeling with the action that caused it. You mind seeks continuous gratification from this action. Therefore, a habit is formed.

Habits that are harmful to your health cause physical changes in your body. Suddenly stopping the habit may cause even further problems, and requires professional intervention. Chronic alcoholics and people addicted to drugs must consult a physician before stopping any of their habits. Life-threatening events may occur from the sudden stoppage of these chemicals.

Hobbies do not cause physical damage to your body, but do cause a financial strain. You may not want to completely eliminate the hobby from your life, especially if it brings you great joy, relaxation and brings you closer to your friends and family. If your hobby brings positivity into your life, it may be more beneficial to hold onto it. You still can find an opportunity to reduce the amount you spend on it. You can keep the hobby and still save money.

Hobbies are important in your life because they provide purpose and can typically be converted into a cash producing venture with imagination and proper motivation. Embrace your creativity and allow it to adapt your hobby into an income-producing activity.

Most habits and hobbies can be broken in the same way. Stopping cold turkey is not an effective method for either and commonly results in the problem area reoccurring in the near future.

You should gradually "lean" yourself off the habit or hobby you desire to quit. Make a plan to gradually use less of the product over the next seven to twenty eight days until you are able to completely stop.

Your body slowly adapts to any changes and typically requires a few weeks to adjust back to normal. Many habits can take up to 28 days to create. Make use out of this strategy by creating good habits to replace those that cost you money or may be harmful to your health.

Cutting habits or reducing their financial impact will not be easy. We are taking a look at every aspect of your finances to seek out areas of opportunity to free up funds to increase your Debt Pay-Down Money balance. Fulfilling plans to reduce or eliminate the cost of habits or hobbies will definitely test your self-control. You will need to stay motivated through the process and stay focused on your final goal. When it comes to breaking a habit, remember why you decided to break it in the first place.

Finally, reward yourself for eliminating a habit or reducing the cost of a hobby. Mentally, it may be one of the hardest things to accomplish without any outside assistance. This deserves a reward.

Identify Your Goals

Importance of Setting Goals

   Your goals are one of the most important aspects to your success. They provide the guidance to get you moving in the right direction the motivation necessary to carry on. Goals will keep you organized in your efforts of achieving financial success and demand action through definite deadlines.

   Your final goal does not have to be the final step. I achieved my initial final goal of eliminating all of my debt, except for my mortgage payment and student loans, and reducing all of my monthly bills and expenses to 50% of our part-time income. Then I realized I could achieve anything I put my mind to; I had aimed too low. This was not a mistake. I had proved to myself that I could succeed and I was ready to take on an even larger challenge. Continue striving for achievement throughout your life.

   Life goals are just as important as your financial ones. Creating these goals is necessary to maintain organization and ensure you don't neglect those important people In your life as you begin to carry out your plans.

Your goals will provide landmarks along your journey. They will keep you organized throughout the process. With your life and finances organized, your journey will be smooth and steady.

How to Set Realistic Goals

In order to guarantee success, you will need to set accurate and obtainable goals. There is a fine balance between these factors. In this lesson, we will show you the methods behind setting realistic goals so you don't set yourself up for failure.

Your goals need to have real and exact figures. For one reason, the accuracy of the information will affect timelines when it comes to creating plans. Another reason is because your mind responds more appropriately to exact figures when it comes to thinking your way to success.

Your goals should be set up to demand consistent action. If you set your deadlines too far away, you will be wasting time, losing momentum, and possibly losing money. On the other hand, if you set the deadline too soon, you will set yourself up for failure and possibly blow any confidence you may have built. Creating too tight of deadlines also has the potential of adding stress to the situation by creating too tight of a budget to live off of comfortably. There is a fine balance when setting deadlines. You want to balance the factors mentioned above with what will fit your personality and risk tolerance.

Your goals should progress in an ascending level of difficulty. As you complete goals which are easier to obtain, you will boost your confidence in the process and be ready to take on more challenging tasks.

Do the math to determine if your goal is realistic. Factor in the payments will be made and the interest that will be added to the balance each month. Mentally work your way from your current situation to the completion of the goal. If the entire equation adds up, there should be no problems with the amounts or deadlines you determined.

To calculate interest on most debt, take the current interest rate percentage (8%) and convert it to a fraction (0.08)

Multiply your month's beginning balance by the interest rate
Example: $10,000 x 0.08 = $800

Divide this balance by 12 months to get the interest rate charged for the current month
Example: $800 ÷ 12 = $66.67

In this scenario, you had a $10,000 balance at the beginning of the month and would be charged an interest fee of $66.67. To predict future interest charges, multiple the interest rate by the anticipated principle balance owed

Understand how it will actually "feel" to proceed through until you reach your goals. Changes in your life may look easy on paper, but the actual process of changing your life can be difficult. Imagine working your way through the steps of your plan, not just focusing on the goal. Imagine living without certain products. How will it feel to go through your routines the way your plan entails? This exercise will help prepare you for the road ahead and give you a strong indicator if your plan is realistic for you.

Your goals should be positive in nature and reflect what you want to have happen in your life. Don't focus on what you don't want. Placing attention on the negative will only draw more of it into your life.

Your goals need to be realistic and obtainable to be practical for use in your debt-elimination strategies. With application of these principles, your progress will be accelerated.

Setting Life Goals

Personally, setting life goals was the most exciting part of the process because it ensured I would get to spend quality time with the people I loved spending time with.

Without organization in your life, your financial plans will eventually fall apart. Take some time and think about the important people in your life. Imagine yourself proceeding through your debt-elimination strategies and get a sense for the time commitment it will require. What people in your life could you not live without? What events or activities do you want to experience with these people?

Create goals to spend a certain amount of time with your friends and family members. Keep in contact with these people and find mutual days off that can spent together. They will be pleased that you went through such great efforts to continue building your relationship, and you will benefit by creating more fulfillment in your life.

The goal is to spend time together; that does not mean you have to spend money, too. There are many cost-effective ways to provide entertainment and enjoy each other's company.

Family activities such as going to the park, taking a hike, or having a family game night at home costs little to nothing. Time spent with friends could include having people over for dinner and a movie. Instead of going to an expensive restaurant, you could mingle at a local coffee house over a beverage. You will need to get creative to keep the costs down to a minimum.

Use the calendar that you filled out earlier as a tool for establishing your life goals. Earlier in the program, you established categories for certain friends and family members. Using the calendar template, fill out the categories at the bottom. For each person, or group of people designated a category, assign the number of days a month you wish to spend with them.

Most people these days have incredibly busy schedules. Without proper planning, it can be difficult to find time to spend with our friends and family. Get in contact with them and use the calendar to coordinate days you can spend together. Using your creativity, or borrowing from the activities list above, plan an event. After the event is planned, mark the day on the calendar.

It is important to follow through with your plans. If for some reason you have to break the plans you made, re-schedule for another day. Your time is already limited, and it can be easy to lose touch with the ones who really fulfill your life. Your life goals are important, and should take priority over your financial goals.

Setting Income-Producing Goals

Increasing your income and finding additional sources of income is the first step to increasing your "Debt Pay-Down Money" balance.

This section, along with the following, will build on the goals you have already developed in the "Foundation Series" of this program.

Work Harder

To increase your income, you could work more hours, find a career that provides increased hours or higher pay, or pick up a second job. I don't know about you, but none of these sound very appealing to me. So, let's search for creative ways to increase your income.

If you have the opportunity to pick up an overtime shift or take on a project for additional income, it may not be a bad idea for a temporary boost in progress or to make up for unexpected expenses. But, it is usually not an effective long-term strategy.

Ask For a Raise

Let's start by taking a look at your current pay rate. Compare this rate to what others in a similar position are receiving. If your compensation falls much shorter than the average, it may be time to ask for a raise.

You may still ask for a raise, even if your pay is equal to that of comparable employees. You will need to prepare a well organized presentation to deliver to your boss. When requesting a raise, it is not sufficient to simply ask for more money than you are currently earning. Your boss has the upper hand in this negotiation and the easy answer in this situation is to just tell you, "No."

There is no such thing as something for nothing. You will need to provide your employer more service in exchange for your increase in pay. This does not mean you have to take on more hours at your job, but you may need to take on more responsibility. Give your employer more than you plan to receive in compensation, and the answer to your request for a raise will be an obvious one.

Ask For a Promotion

Depending on the relationships you have built with your co-workers and management, your time with the company, and your skill set, you may be able to request a promotion.

The first step in planning for promotion is to understand the position you are seeking. Know the ins and outs. Speak to people who are already in the position and watch how they do their job. Your employer will feel more confident placing you in a position that you completely understand and are still willing to take.

The next step is to perform additional duties at your current level. These additional duties should be the same or similar to those of the position you desire. Show your employer that you are willing to take on the extra responsibility. When you are at work, act as if you are already in the higher position. This will build your employer's trust and confidence in your abilities to be successful if promoted.

Finally, ask for an interview. Let the management team know that you desire to move up in the company and are ready to take the next step.

If you don't get the interview, you will still stand out as a promising choice for the company's future. Continue building their confidence and build your relationships within the company.

Be ready for an interview. If you build enough trust in your employer, and the time is right, they will give you the opportunity to really sell yourself. This is your time to seal the deal. Be confident in your abilities and sell yourself.

Sell Your Skills

An exercise that is beneficial at determining where you can produce additional income is to make a list of your hobbies, achievements, and skills. From this list, find a specialty or product you can offer someone else in the form of a side business.

A specialty could be as simple as cleaning house. There are many busy professionals who either do not have the time or do not care to spend their free time cleaning their own house.

You can also turn a hobby into a side business. Your creativity could be profitable with some imagination. Designing scarves, making quilts, and building dog houses or bird houses are some examples of items people may be interested in purchasing. If you are a tech expert, you may find additional income in designing websites or solving people's computer problems. You could sell the items in front of your house, in the classifieds, at the local farmers market, or online.

Many people sell their skill set online by becoming a virtual assistant. A virtual assistant can advertise their abilities on sites such as Odesk.com and Elance.com. You set your own wages and choose which jobs to accept.

Once you find your talent, begin advertising your name with your circle of friends, co-workers and family members. These are the people who know you best, like you, and trust you. They will be your best immediate customers. Let them know of your services and ask them to refer you to their friends and family. It is a win-win for everybody; your customers get a cost-effective service or product and you get extra money for your talents.

Sell Your Stuff

Another form of producing income is to sell items you already own. Go through your house, garage, shed or storage unit and begin gathering the items that you no longer use and have no need for.

The next step is to determine how you want to sell the items. Research the items and come up with a price for each. You can take a weekend and host a yard sale or list the items individually by placing them on a free online classifieds website such as Craigslist.

If you are more concerned about the price you wish to receive for the item, the online classifieds will be a better option. If you wish to sell the item quick at a discounted rate, then go with a yard sale. Advertising for a yard sale is as simple as placing a sign near the closest main route near your neighborhood to direct traffic to your location. I had best luck with listing the main items I had available, such as "Baby Clothes" or "Tools Available."

Selling items around your house that you no longer need will reduce clutter, keep you better organized, and therefore reduce stress.

Write down your new income-producing goals on your "Financial Goals and Plan" worksheet and update your "Income Organization" worksheet as money starts rolling in. Finally, keep your "Financial Balance" worksheet up to date to show your progress and help drive your motivation.

Setting Spending-Reduction Goals

  Finding ways to reduce your spending can majorly impact how fast your goals are accomplished. By taking sacrifices now through reducing or eliminating spending, you will achieve your goals quicker and really begin to live life to the fullest. In the "Foundation Series," you categorized your spending as either "Essential" or "Non-Essential."

  Earlier in this program, you prioritized each item purchased using the "Spending Priority" worksheet, and added the total cost of spending in each priority level.

  Now, you will choose whether to keep spending money on the item, reduce your spending, or eliminate it. Here is a simple, emotionless approach to this method:

Priority Level	Action
1 – 2 (Low)	Eliminate any spending
3 – 8 (Medium)	Reduce spending
9 – 10 (High)	None to minor changes in spending

Eliminating spending using this method takes emotion out of the decision, and can make decision-making easier.

Take a quick look at the low priority items you blindly decided to eliminate. Do you see any issues with your decision? Is this a decision you could live with? Now, add up the total money you will save each month after eliminating these low priority spending items. Determine if this strategy will work for you.

When emotion is taken out of the equation, and you only look at the numbers, the decision can come easier. Ultimately, this is your strategy and you get to make the final decisions.

With that said, let's take a look at some ideas for reducing or eliminating spending. The more money you can free up, the larger your "Debt Pay-Down Money" balance will grow. The items have been categorized into major spending groups:

Food

Food is required for survival, and therefore is labeled an "Essential Spending" item. Just because an item is labeled essential does not mean its cost cannot be reduced. We will explore some cost-effective strategies.

Have you ever gone to the grocery store in search of only a couple items and left with a cart full of groceries? Have you ever had food go bad before you had a chance to eat it? Is there food sitting on your shelf unwanted by the members of your household?

An excellent solution to all three of these problems is a meal plan. To create a meal plan, make a list of the recipes you enjoy cooking and the family enjoys eating. Try and focus on those with simple ingredients. Come up with enough meals for a one to two week period.

Next, take an inventory of your kitchen and find out what ingredients you will need to make the meal plan happen.

Finally, go to the store and purchase those items necessary to complete the meals. Keep track of the recipe card so you remember what ingredients go to which meal.

Make a list of the meals you are ready to prepare for the week and place it on the fridge. You can do this with our "Meal Plan" organizer, which can be downloaded for free at SAHDLife.com/DebtForms. This organizer will establish what days the meals will be prepared and displays the left over's that are still available. Now, every time you go to the kitchen and wonder what there is to eat, you will have the information front and center.

This plan will help eliminate wasted food, and save you money from unnecessary repeated trips to the grocery store.

Every Sunday before I began my next shift rotation, I would cook multiple meals and place them in individual containers. This helped organize my time more efficiently during my workweek and saved us a large amount of money.

I would bring these prepared meals to work for my lunch and dinner. Working 12 hour shifts on the ambulance required me to be creative in my methods. I had no access to a fridge, so I had to bring one refrigerated meal for lunch and one frozen meal for dinner. I had no personal microwave, so I would have to use one at a local convenient store or at the hospital's medic lounge. The amount of money saved over going out to eat or finding a meal at the hospital cafeteria was substantial. And, it was convenient to be able to grab a healthy meal that could be heated in only a couple minutes.

Plan to bring lunch to work. Find creative recipes that will heat easily. When you cook amazing recipes and take the leftovers with you to your job, you will not only save money and be excited about lunch time, but you will also make your co-workers a little jealous.

If you are serious about saving money, you need to stop going out to eat at restaurants. The same meal you would purchase at a restaurant for $15 a plate plus tip can be prepared at home for under $2 per serving.

If going out to eat is something that fulfils your life, then you could find other areas to cut expenses. But, if you can live without it, it should be reserved for a reward or special occasion only.

A good investment may be to enroll in a local cooking class. You will learn tips and tricks to create outstanding meals, gain confidence in cooking various types of foods, and save money in the long run with your newly developed skills.

Coffee

Depending on who you talk to, coffee may end up under the "Essential" or the "Non-Essential" category. I am not here to judge you by your categorization; I am here to offer some suggestions on reducing the monthly cost of your coffee.

A simple way to reduce the amount spent at the coffee stand is to limit the number of times you go. If you buy seven coffees a week, you could try limiting yourself to five. At nearly $5 a coffee, you would find a savings of $40 a month from this category alone with minimal sacrifice.

A slightly cheaper alternative to the coffee stand is to purchase bottled coffee from a convenience store or grocery store. These bottled coffees have similar taste to an iced latté and cost around $1 to $2 less than the ones prepared for you in person. Over the span of a month, if consumed one a day, you would see an average savings of $45.

I made a delicious flavored iced latté at home using micro-ground coffee packets, flavored syrup, and milk. These drinks taste very similar to the coffee stand and saved me $112.50 each month!

Habits

The habits we are focusing on in this section are poor for your health and/or cost you money. They are considered habits if you use the product on a regular basis or crave its use. If this section does not apply to you, feel free to skip it. Otherwise, I will share with you my thoughts on the matter.

There is no better time than now to quit. If you have an unhealthy habit that you wish to stop, you should seek professional services in that area. They will be able to provide you with the proper resources and health considerations when it comes time to stop using the substance.

In this lesson, I will share some reasons that may persuade you to either quit or reduce the use to a healthier and affordable amount.

In the United States, smokers spend an average of $180 a month on cigarettes at a pack a day rate. Drinkers spend an average of $100 a month on alcohol at 2 drinks a day. Tobacco users spend an average of $150 a month at a can a day.

Tobacco use has been associated with many types of cancers and alcohol use has been connected with liver failure, diabetes, and kidney damage.

The point is that these substances are harmful to your body, especially when used in excess, and will lead to terminal conditions. In choosing this program, you have decided you want to live a long, fulfilled life with the freedom and ability to do what you want. You have determined you want to spend it with those most important to you.

Think about your family and friends. Consider those who care about you the most and cherish their time with you. Now, imagine that all of this was taken away because of your unhealthy habits. Imagine how your friends and family would feel having lost you early in life.

On the ambulance, I have seen these substances cause misery in many people's lives. Please do yourself a favor and reduce the amount you use, if not eliminate it permanently. You will not only see more money in your pockets in the end, but more importantly, you will live a longer, healthier, and happier life.

Entertainment

Entertainment items may be one of the hardest categories to break spending habits. People spend good money entertaining themselves, as it has come to an understanding that entertainment always costs money.

It would not be practical to say that you must cut all entertainment until you are out of debt. Doing so would lead to one boring life and would not reinforce the values of this program.

There are many options for free or cheap entertainment. Take a look at the local attractions in your area and find the ones that offer free or affordable choices.

You could host a party at your place. Have friends over for dinner, host a game night, or rent a movie and invite people over for "Popcorn and a Flick." You could take the family to a park, have a picnic, go on a walk through town, or find an exciting trail to hike.

My wife and I would actually go to our gym's pool to entertain ourselves by going swimming. This did not cost us any more than the membership and gave us an added benefit. It almost felt like we were on vacation at a hotel.

Many businesses offer free or reduced admission during certain days or specific times. The Children's Hands-On Museum in my area offered a free admission one day a month. Many museums offer the same. Some theaters offer discounted admission before noon. You will need to get creative and do some research in your specific area to find some real deals.

Clothing

Reducing the cost of clothing starts with the store you shop at. To begin, you should stop shopping at the mall. You can find similar clothing for much less outside of the department stores.

This does not mean you are going to buy your clothing second hand from the thrift shop. You can find the same brands, same quality, and similar styles at discount clothing stores such as Ross and TJ Maxx.

My wife and I found the majority of our clothing at these stores. There are special occasions that we would indulge and go to the mall, but the majority of our shopping occurred at these discount stores.

Many of our children's clothing items were given to us as gifts from their grandparents. The clothes we bought were usually purchased through higher-end second hand stores.

We decided to purchase our kids clothing through second hand stores for three reasons: First, they were growing so fast that they didn't fit in the clothing sizes very long. Second, because of this fact, the second hand clothing was lightly used if not brand new. Some items still had the original tag on them! Third, we were able to sort through the clothing options and find those that fit our standard for quality and cleanliness. When the kids no longer fit in these outfits, we returned them to the same store for either store credit or a check.

There are many ways to save money on your clothing and still look good. You must stay presentable to sustain a job, maintain your social status, and hold your self-esteem high. Dig into your creative side and find methods to save in this category.

Household Items

This is a broad category that can include anything from decorations and other aesthetic improvements to maintenance and repairs.

Your home is your castle and decorating it may be important in your enjoyment of life. Consider your goals when it comes to purchasing items of aesthetic value. As with any purchase, it pays to shop around and find the best deal. My wife and I found many great household items at the same stores we bought our clothing. Ross and TJ Maxx offer many items to decorate your house at reasonable prices. We were able to brighten up our home and make it feel warm and welcome without breaking the bank.

If you are in need of furniture, and trying to stay within budget, you may find used items through an online classifieds website such as Craigslist. We were able to find brand new furniture items at Big Lots. Many of our major furniture items came from this store and we still receive complements on their look and feel. People are usually surprised to hear where it came from, but once they experience it, they are believers.

Repairs and maintenance on your home can add up to large totals, especially if you hire a contractor to do the work. To start, if you rent your home, repairs will most likely be paid for by the landlord. Tenant-Landlord Laws protect the tenant in situations where repairs are required for the house to be maintained in a livable condition. Consult your local laws or an attorney for more details.

If you own your home, the burden of repairs and maintenance falls on you. When faced with a repair, first determine if you can perform the work yourself. Do not let the lack of tools get in the way of deciding whether to do it yourself or hire a contractor. Many times, it is much cheaper to buy the tool than it is to hire the professional. The added benefit is that you get to add another tool to your toolbox.

If you need conviction that the project will be cheaper if done yourself, call a contractor out to your property for a free estimate. Compare the cost of buying the tools and fixing it yourself versus hiring professional help. The difference is usually substantial.

If you have the time and the skill to perform the job yourself, you will save a lot of money. If not, you may know someone who has the skills necessary.

So, what happens if you don't have the mechanical skills and don't know anyone else who does either? The next best choice to do is to hire a contractor to perform the "hard work" only. There are many jobs that you can perform. Most jobs require some sort of prep work before the "hard work" begins. Let your contractor know that you are looking to cut costs by helping out with easier tasks. Ask for an estimate if you assist in the completion of the project.

As with any contracted work, be sure and get estimates from three different contractors. This will ensure you get the best deal possible when hiring a professional.

When you receive the estimate, make sure it details exactly what work you will be completing and what your contractor will be doing.

I had a septic problem in a brand new house that we bought through a foreclosure sale. I knew nothing about septic systems, so I called a professional. I was told that the problem would require $2000 to fix. They explained that the cost could increase if further problems were discovered.

I did not schedule an appointment. After calling multiple companies and hearing the same figures, I decided to seek expert advice from my family and friends. Little did I know, my neighbor worked for the water department and was familiar with similar pumps found in septic systems. He helped me pull the old pump out and found a crack in the housing.

We replaced the cheap, plastic pump with a cast iron replacement. He was able to get me a discount on the supplies using a distributer he was familiar with through his workplace. In the end, the fix only cost me $330 plus a "Thank You" case of beer.

Automobile

The cost of your automobile, in this lesson on spending, includes fuel, repairs, and accessories. The actual cost of your vehicle will be covered in the monthly debt section.

Your fuel costs may be a major expense each month. There is not much you can do about the cost of fuel driving to and from work, unless you change your vehicle or change your job.

There are small steps you can take to ensure you are getting the best mileage out of your car or truck. Make sure you have an appropriate tire pressure and keep your vehicles maintenance up to date. Your driving habits also have an effect on your gas mileage. To save on fuel you need to make soft accelerations, avoid unnecessary braking, and try to maintain a consistent speed on the freeway. Avoiding unnecessary use of the air conditioner will also help you gain additional miles per gallon.

Simple vehicle repairs can be performed by you, or someone you know who has worked on vehicles before. Simple repairs, such as changing the oil, fixing the brakes, rotating tires, maintaining critical fluids, and other basic maintenance can be done at home with relative ease. If you don't know how to perform these skills, you may know a friend or family member who can teach you. You may also hire this person to do the work for you.

I had a family member who was excellent at working on vehicles and saved me thousands in repair costs. We rewarded him and his wife by paying for their annual family trip to Leavenworth.

If you cannot perform the repair, and don't have any personal auto mechanic resources, your next best option is to take your vehicle to a certified auto mechanic.

A cheap alternative to getting major fixes done at a business is to take it to the local college or vocational school. Many of these schools offer auto mechanic courses and may be willing to work on your car. These places are looking for participants who need repairs on their vehicle and are willing to let students perform the work under the supervision of an expert.

Rest assured that the fixes are monitored by an expert instructor. Most auto shops are run by mechanics, but how many of them do you think could also teach a class on the subject? Weigh the risks and benefits and decide for yourself what you are comfortable with.

You may want to research the cost of public transportation. You may find that you are able to commute to and from work at a more affordable price. Factor in the price of gas and maintenance into your decision. Your commute time will most likely increase, but you will have more free time to accomplish personal tasks. Just think of what you could get done while sitting on the light rail or bus each day. If you decide public transportation is appropriate for your plans, your next decision is whether to keep your car or sell it. If you currently have multiple cars, you may find you can live with only one vehicle.

Summary

This program is about thinking outside the box. Keep up the creativity as you work on reducing the cost of your spending. If there is one point that should be drawn from this lesson, it is that "intellectual currency," or the money saved from your creative ideas, is far more valuable than physical currency, and takes a whole lot less effort to earn. In one simple thought, you can save hundreds of dollars. It would take hours of physical labor to make the same amount in cash.

When you come across a major expense, such as a home or auto repair, take a step back and analyze the problem. Clear your mind and come up with a creative solution to fix the problem. Every expense has a cost-effective alternative. Some may be obvious and others may need searching.

Never stop looking for ways to reduce your spending. There are always new and exciting ways you can still enjoy life while reducing its daily cost. Every dollar counts and will get you closer to your goals of financial success.

Write down your new and revised spending-reduction goals on your "Financial Goals and Plan" worksheet, and update your "Financial Balance" worksheet.

Setting Debt-Reduction Goals

Getting out of debt is about eliminating your bills as fast as possible. Finding ways to reduce or eliminate your debt now, before you spend your hard earned money paying down the balance, will get you to your final goal faster than you ever imagined.

Reducing your debts will require effective negotiation skills. These skills can be easily acquired and developed through practical application.

When negotiating, you should be aware of your opponent's position and the options they have at their disposal. This will allow you to anticipate any counteroffer and gives you time to prepare. You will also be aware of who has the upper hand in the process. Typically, the side with the upper hand has less to lose and is in more of a position to call the shots during the process.

To be effective, you want to know how your opponent could benefit from your proposition. This is especially true if you enter the negation without having the upper hand. Paint the picture of your offer with the best interest of your opponent. By creating a win-win scenario, you will have no problem finding a "Yes."

Keep an open mind as you proceed through this lesson. Do not immediately dismiss an idea until you have explored "How can I make this work?" Each strategy in reducing debt is geared toward increasing your "Debt Pay-Down Money" balance.

Subscription Services

Subscription services include products which require a monthly payment to remain active. These may include streaming movie rentals, magazine subscriptions, TV and internet plans, and rent-to-own agreements.

You have the option to stop payment at any time, and therefore stop receiving the service or product. Subscriptions are the easiest type of debt to eliminate. Simply inform the company of your intent to cancel and they will stop collecting money from you each month. This is a no-hassle way to keep more money in your pocket each month.

It may be more difficult to reduce the cost of a subscription, but not impossible. Some savvy business owners understand that it is better to keep a customer and collect something than to collect nothing at all.

If you are not willing to separate from your subscription service, but also want to save money, you may be able to negotiate a better deal. Begin by researching the competition's prices. Next, give your company a call and let them know you are planning on stopping service. You can either tell them it has become too much for you to afford, or you found a better offer from their competitor. Ask if there is a cheaper alternative to your current plan, or if there is anything they can do to make their product more affordable. The worst that can happen is they tell you "No" and you stay with the service at the current price.

Let the company know you are ready to stop service, but would be willing to continue in exchange for a better deal. More often than not, you will find some sort of discount or bonus. This is "intellectual currency" at work!

If you are willing to part from the service, simply call and cancel.

Contracts

Services purchased on a contract will be difficult to negotiate, because the terms of the deal have already been locked into place. These purchases may include cell phone plans, TV and internet plans, and gym memberships.

If you are looking to eliminate the service, you will need to continue making payments until your contract ends. The first thing you should do is review the agreement or contact the company to confirm your contracted end date.

If you wish to keep service with your current provider, but reduce its cost, you will have to do some negotiating at the time of signing the renewal contract. The time you have between now and the end of your contracted period should be used to research competitors prices and develop a negotiation strategy. Remember to find a win-win scenario.

Be prepared to switch your service over to a competitor if your company does not give in to your proposal.

The growing popularity of cell phones has resulted in an ever growing cost of cell phone providers. I was able to save hundreds of dollars by switching my phone service to a pre-paid company.

The pre-paid company offered a variety of phones with unlimited nationwide calls, unlimited text messages, and unlimited data for a low monthly payment of $45. There was never any worry of going over on our data limits or paying overage charges. In fact, I was able to tether my cell phone to my laptop or create a Wi-Fi hotspot for internet use on other devices.

The leading carriers were charging $90 a month for service that only included 2GB of data. To me, the choice was simple. Between my wife and me, we were saving $90 a month. I was willing to sacrifice having the latest phone to accelerate my progress in achieving my final goal sooner.

TV companies offer multiple deals, but may only advertise their most profitable. You may need to do some digging around to find the best deal through your provider. If you are not willing to completely part from TV while you work to accomplish your financial goals, you could compromise with less selection on your TV line up.

Most channel packages offered include all of the basic and extended channels. I called my provider and asked what the cheapest option was and they told me I currently had it. I stayed persistent and continued requesting a more affordable option. I was finally told there was a very basic package which only offered a few channels, but the representative assured me the lineup was limited and would not be beneficial. These channels covered most of the news, sports, and sitcom shows I enjoyed, so I went ahead with the offer. The cost was about half of what I was currently paying.

Services

Monthly services may include utilities such as electricity, water, sewer and garbage, auto insurance, and home or renters insurance.

There is no way to completely stop your auto insurance unless you want to get rid of your car. If this is not an option, then the next best thing is to reduce its cost.

The best way to reduce the cost of these bills is through effective negotiation. Rates are always changing between companies, so research the competition will be your most effective strategy in obtaining the best deal.

Many companies, especially home and auto insurance providers, increase the cost of your service gradually over time in hopes that you, the customer, will not notice the change or give it any concern. Their competitor is always looking for new customers and is usually willing to offer a discount to earn your business.

Take advantage of this. Call the competition and ask for price quotes. Once you have the competitor's prices organized, and you know exactly what services you get for that price, it is time to call your provider and inform them you will be stopping service.

Typically, they will transfer you to someone who specializes in retaining customers. Do not be shy in explaining your intentions. Your goal here is to get a discount on the services you are probably paying too much for.

Tell your company you are leaving for a better offer with the competition. Give them the name of the competitor and the price they are offering. Finish by asking if there is anything that can be done on their end to beat that deal and earn your continued business.

If your current provider does not budge, then transfer your services to their competition at a cheaper price. It is in your best interest to keep your bills as low as possible, especially if the lower rate includes the same service. If your current provider gives in by offering a discount, then sign up for the service at the reduced price.

Your next step is to call the cheapest competitor back. Inform them that your current provider has just beaten their offer. See if they are willing to reduce their price further to earn your business. This trend can continue until one side is unwilling to reduce their prices any further.

I had successfully reduced my auto insurance bill from $167 a month to $112 by getting the two companies to bid against each other. I did so without losing any coverage options I had prior. With only a few phone calls, I had created $55 a month out of thin air.

Garbage services typically include multiple options, including container size and frequency of pick-up, which vary in price. Give your provider a call and explore these options. If you do not fill your can every week, you may be more suited for a bi-weekly pickup schedule or a smaller trash receptacle. Many counties offer a discount for recycling. Make sure this is added to your plan. It is good for the environment and good for your wallet.   Another option is to take your trash to the dump yourself. This will require more time and effort, but could save you some well needed money.

 If you have central heat, maintaining a constant temperature is usually more cost effective than turning heaters on and off constantly. If your rooms have individual wall heaters, you can close doors and turn down the heat in rooms that are unused. Large baseboard heaters draw power off your home's 240 volt supply almost constantly. These heaters stay on for long periods of time and will substantially increase the cost of your electricity bill.

Your local hardware store will have employees who are knowledgeable in techniques to reduce the cost of your utilities. They are an excellent resource to reach out to.

Loan Installments

Installment payments on loans are typically used to purchase major items, such as an automobile, but also can be used to purchase many smaller items, such as using a credit card. These bills may also include medical and student loan debt.

These loans have a total balance due, consisting of a principle balance plus any interest accumulated. The repayment schedule is typically set up for monthly payments over the life of the loan. These loans are sometimes secured by collateral, or an item of cash value. The ones that aren't are called unsecured loans

We will sub-categorize specific loan installment examples below for your convenience:

Automobile

Car payments are may be the next most expensive monthly payment after mortgage or rent. If you don't own your car outright, or are not set up to have it paid off in the next year with minimum payments alone, you should consider selling it.

This is where most people stop and begin to focus on the reasons why something *won't* work. As you know, most cars are not an investment and people typically owe more than the car is worth. A common response I hear to this strategy is, "I can't sell my car, because I owe more than I could get for it."

My wife and I had two brand new cars when we were at the peak of our debt. Our payments, plus the cost of full-coverage insurance totaled near $1000 a month! We had typical mid-class vehicles and just the base models. After totaling our car payments, we thought, "We could own another house for the amount we are paying on our cars alone!" I loved my new car when I had purchased it, but the burden of debt eventually made me resent it.

This sparked an idea that would take us further than we imagined. It happened to be one of the most beneficial moves in our financial strategy. We decided to sell our vehicles and purchase cheaper models.

We took a loss on selling the cars; over $2000 initially. We paid for this loss with the next month's anticipated car loan and insurance payment, and borrowed the rest of the money from a family member. We developed a plan to pay the borrowed money back in less than two months, and we delivered on our promise.

We survived off one vehicle for a short period of time and eventually found the perfect replacement. We ended up purchasing the same car, but ten years older.

The process worked so well that we decided to repeat it with our second vehicle. The switch from brand new cars to more affordable, but reliable vehicles saved us nearly $450 a month! Within six months, we had one of the cars paid in full.

We did a lot of research into the reliability of certain vehicles and limited our search to those specific models. We only settled on a purchase when we believed we had found the best deal possible. We bought my wife's car through a wholesale auto dealer who listed it under bluebook. My car was 13 years old and had less than 55,000 miles. Good deals are out there, but you have to be ready to jump on them when they present themselves.

In the end, the move to sell our cars for the older model saved us $19,500 over a 3 year period. This included the loss we took initially.

As we shared our goals of selling the brand new cars to get older ones, we were warned that the older vehicles we were about to buy would probably break down often and cost us more in maintenance. I don't know about you, but I don't see a vehicle costing more than $19,500 in maintenance and repairs, no matter how old it is.

I reassured myself that I was making the right decision by doing some research on major repairs. The cost to replace an engine or transmission would run around $2000 - $4000. Even if I had to replace the engine and transmission on both vehicles, I would still be saving money. Of course, if this were to happen, I would be better off selling the car for scrap parts and purchasing another used vehicle as a replacement for even less.

When researching a used vehicle to purchase, determine a price range you are willing to spend. Then, find the most reliable vehicle that will keep you under budget. Consider gas mileage as you make your new selection, as this may become another factor in saving money.

If selling your vehicle does not fit into your plans, you could consider refinancing the loan. Search the competition and find a lower interest rate. You will begin to see benefit in refinancing your auto loan with a drop in interest rate by at least 1%. Additional fees may be rolled into the balance of your loan when you refinance, so you will want to make sure the benefits outweigh the risks.

You may also have the option to extend the life of the loan to free up additional money which can be applied toward your "Debt Pay-Down Money" balance.

When refinancing, it may appear you will be paying more interest on your loan. If you do not stick with your debt-elimination strategy, you will be. By extending the loan and lowering the minimum payment, you are actually borrowing money from that loan's minimum payment to be applied toward the payoff of a higher priority debt in your strategy. You will pay off bills and increase your "Debt Pay-Down Money" balance faster using these strategies. But, you must be persistent with your strategy, otherwise you risk placing yourself in a worse financial position in the long run.

Depending on your situation, you may be able to sell your vehicle and use public transportation. If your family has the ability to function with one vehicle, or if your situation allows for none, this may be an option for you to consider.

When my wife and I lived in Colorado, I was driving 45 minutes to work and my gas bill alone was $450 a month. I was able to cut expenses by riding a bike to the light rail station, taking it downtown Denver, and then riding the remaining 9 miles into Aurora where I worked. The trip only added 30 minutes commute each way. I enjoyed the benefit of being able to read on the train and exercise every day on my bike. I also was able to save $350 a month.

Credit Card

Credit card debt can be managed fairly easy. The easiest method is to transfer the balance of your current card to one with a lower interest rate. Visit credit unions and banks in your area and ask for information on the credit cards they offer. Let them know you are looking to transfer your balance to their card as long as you can get a better interest rate.

Another useful resource can be found online. There are many sites that advertise credit cards and allow you to search for the perk you are most interested in. You can narrow your search to those cards with low APR and low fees on balance transfers. Either visit CreditCards.com, or search "Credit cards with low balance transfer rate."

There are a few things you should understand when it comes to balance transfers. You can transfer the balance from the credit card you have now to one with a lower interest rate for little or no cost. Some companies roll in an additional percentage of the balance that was actually transferred to new card. This is typically 3%. You should be aware that the interest rate may be fixed or adjustable. Adjustable rate APR means your interest rate may fluctuate, which could increase the monthly payments due and cost you more money in the end. There may be an introductory rate offered for a specific amount of time. Unless you plan to have the balance paid in full before this offer expires, you will need to account for the future rate increase and understand how it will affect your goals.

You should also be aware that interest rates can change at any time, regardless of whether it is fixed or not. This right given to the credit card companies is buried deep within the fine print of the credit card agreement. In this instance, you will receive a notice of rate increase in the mail. To avoid the inevitable interest rate hike, you have two options: you can close the account and keep the original interest rate or transfer your balance to a new card or loan.

You should consult an expert at the bank institution to get information on any additional hidden fees or other variables that could affect you financially.

I had a credit card with a fixed rate of 12% and a balance of $9500. With a little research, I found that the credit union where I currently banked was offering a credit card at 6% variable APR and no fee on balance transfer. The interest rate could change every quarter, or 3 months. This simple transfer saved me $50 a month in interest. Since our plan had us paying off the card in less than 4 months, I was not worried about the variable interest rate.

If your goal is to have your credit card paid off in the next 6 months or sooner, you may consider transferring your balance to a card with an introductory offer of 0% APR on balance transfers. Typically these promotional offers expire after 6 months, where your current account balance will begin to accumulate interest charges. If you plan to have the account paid in full prior to this offer expiring, you will not pay interest on the remaining length the account is open.

Student Loans

Student loan debt is similar to most other loan installments, but earns its own category due to some unique variables. As with other loan installments, student loans have a principle balance that needs to be paid in full to satisfy the loan.

The difference is, student loan debt may be treated differently during a bankruptcy situation, and there are also programs available where student loan debt may be forgiven.

Filing for bankruptcy may reduce or eliminate certain debts. This does not necessarily apply to your student loan debt. Filing for bankruptcy is damaging enough to your credit, but if you have federal student loan debt, you may still be responsible for payments.

Getting out of debt is hard work, but the reward at the end is worth it! The skills you acquire on your journey will allow you to achieve things in your life you only dreamed of. To successfully stay out of debt and live life to the fullest, you must go through the process of education and practical application. It is all a part of developing your mindset to one of success and prosperity.

You could have a case that repayment of your student loan debt would cause such a hardship that you would be unable to pay future financial obligations, but this is rarely awarded in courts. In the debt rescue program, we work to improve your current financial situation where you can avoid bankruptcy completely and get out of debt without assistance.

Federal Loan Forgiveness programs are available which offer to eliminate the remaining portion of student loan debt if certain qualifications are met. First, you must be working for a government or non-profit public service agency involved in law enforcement, public health, or similar fields. Second, you must have made at least 120 on time payments, or 10 years payment history, to be considered. The government may place additional stipulations, such as requiring you work in rural area or attend to specific ethnic regions.

Additional information about this program, and the options you have available for your student loan debt can be found at the government student loan website: Studentaid.ed.gov.

Just like any other installment loan, you have the option to refinance your student loans to achieve a lower interest rate or extend the length of the loan. Most student loans are placed on a 20 year repayment cycle, so there may not be any more room for an extension on your payment plan. Remember, the goal is to free up as much money as possible so it can be applied to your highest priority debt.

Refer to the "Loan Installment" section for more details on refinancing that apply to your student loans.

Medical Bill

After a medical bill is processed by your insurance company, any remaining balance is sent to you in the form of a lump-sum payment due.

You may be able to reduce the burden of this bill by placing it on a no interest repayment plan. Most medical bills can be placed on these payment plans if you explain a financial hardship and help develop a plan to make monthly payments. This can be a life-saver if an unexpected medical problem arises.

You may also qualify for financial assistance. I had a medical bill from the emergency room that totaled over $2500 after insurance had processed the claim. I had considered filing for assistance, but was told by co-workers that there was no way I would qualify due to my salary. One person, who made almost half of my salary, told me he didn't even attempt to get financial assistance because it would have been a "waste of time."

I ended up filing for the aid anyways, and had my debt reduced by 50%. One simple phone call is all it took. This move saved me $1250 on an unexpected expense.

You don't know your potential until you try. Weigh the risks and benefits. If the only risk is spending the time on the phone with the company or filling out paperwork, then I would say the benefit far outweighs the risk. Give it a shot. You may surprise yourself and everyone else in the end.

Mortgage

Your mortgage is most likely your single largest expense each month. House payments take up to half of a person's income. Depending on your situation, you have multiple options available. Each option varies in risks involved and should be carefully considered and fully understood before putting into practice.

If you are able to make your payments without difficulty, and are not currently behind on payments, you may consider refinancing. There are many options available when you refinance. Your goal is to free up additional money to add to your "Debt Pay-Down Money" balance, so you will want to extend the loan to 30 years or more.

Contact your mortgage consultant for more information on refinancing. By extending the loan back to 30 years or more, and possibly lowering the interest rate, you will reduce your monthly payment. The money saved each month be added to your "Debt Pay-Down Money" balance, and will be applied straight toward the highest priority debt in your strategy. Only extend your mortgage if you include paying it off as part of your strategy. We will discuss less aggressive approaches to your mortgage in the Articles section.

Your goal, while implementing Debt Rescue's debt-elimination strategy, is to free up as much money as possible to pay off smaller debts until you reach the largest one. Don't worry; it won't take you 30+ years to pay off your mortgage.

When you refinance, do not pull cash out from your equity. Pulling cash from one loan to pay off others is a form of debt-consolidation. This strategy only multiplies your problems by adding two or more payments into one large debt. This makes you responsible for the larger minimum payment covering multiple debts and does not allow you to take advantage of maximizing your "Debt Pay-Down Money."

If you are above water in your mortgage, meaning you are current on payments, and the house is worth more than you owe, you have the option to sell. After selling your house you could either purchase a more affordable home or rent a house or apartment for cheaper than your current monthly payments. You have three options to consider when it comes to selling: you can sell with a realtor, sell by owner, or sell with seller financing.

When you sell your house using a realtor, you will need to factor in the realtor's fees. Most will take their commission at the time the house is sold. Realtors will be able to determine an appropriate listing price and determine your profit or loss after closing costs and realtor fees are factored. They will take care of putting the house on the market, advertising your property, scheduling showings and bring potential buyers through the house during showings. Their team deals with all the legal paperwork and processes the documents through escrow.

If you are up for the challenge, you may consider 'For sale by owner.' When you sell your own home, you do all of the work yourself. You take care of all the contracts and legal documents, list the property, advertise, answer phone calls, schedule showings and take the prospective buyers through the property. In the end, you get to pay yourself by keeping the 6% commission you would have paid a realtor. It does take a much larger time commitment.

Do some research before taking on the task of selling a home. Sales contracts can be found online or through office supply stores. You should also consult with an escrow and title company as they may have documents for you to use in your transaction. Begin advertising your home by placing a "For Sale" sign out front. Another excellent source of free advertising is the free online classified sites. There are plenty of resources online that specialize in owners who wish to sell their homes themselves. Search for a "For Sale by Owner" website. Some of these resources provide packages that include all of the instructions and documents you will need to get started and complete the transaction.

Selling your house with seller financing involves more risk, but may be beneficial. Some buyers, especially these days, do not have the credit to obtain a loan through the banks. This may also be an alternative way to sell if you owe more than the house is worth.

In this scenario, you would rent your house for a pre-determined time, typically three years, and include an option to purchase contract. This is also called a rent-to-own or a lease option.

During this three year period, the tenant/buyer can repair their credit and "test drive" the house to make sure it is a good fit for purchase. If the tenant/buyer has been diligent in repairing their credit, they can purchase your house with a standard mortgage.

You will need two contracts to perform a rent-to-own transaction: the rental contract and a separate option to purchase contract. To obtain these contracts, search online, go to your local office supply store, or consult a real estate attorney.

Before you attempt this option, you will need to see if the numbers make sense to your specific situation. Begin by verifying the median rent in your area. You can consult a property management company, call landlords who have similar properties listed nearby, or use the online tool: Rentometer.com.

With an option to purchase contract, you may be able to ask for more in rent each month than your area's median rate. This is because typically a few hundred dollars a month gets credited back toward the purchase of the house when the buyer exercises their option to purchase. This credit is typically referred to as "Rent Credits."

After figuring out the median rent in the area, with consideration of adding additional "Rent Credit" each month, you will be able to determine if a rent-to-own option is possible. If you are able to collect more money each month than your mortgage payment, then the deal has potential.

On signing the deal with your new buyer, you will collect an "Option Deposit" in addition to your "Security Deposit." The security deposit is a reserve the tenant funds in case any damage is caused to the unit during tenancy. The Option deposit is the money paid for having the option to purchase your home in the future. This money is typically applied toward the purchase when your buyer decides to buy the house, but it is also non-refundable if the buyer backs out of the purchase for any reason.

There are a few risks to consider. First, you will be renting to a tenant for possibly three years. The tenants may not purchase the house and they could damage the place. Second, you are still responsible for the mortgage payment, even if you do not receive rent from the tenant. Third, renting out your house will still affect your debt to income ratio.

This will affect your ability to purchase a second home through a bank, but not necessarily your ability to rent.

Another option is to rent your house. You can rent the entire house to a family and find a cheaper stay for yourself, or you could rent a segment of your house and continue living in it.

Renting your house is similar to the rent-to-own strategy mentioned above, except you will not include an option to buy. This could be a short-term strategy for reducing your housing costs while you implement your strategies if you don't want to lose your house in the process.

First, determine how long it will take for you to achieve your goals. This will be the timeframe you are looking to rent your house. After your goals are achieved, you can move back into your home or purchase a new one and use the rental as an investment.

You can rent the house yourself, or use the services of a professional property management company. If you decide to use property management to handle your rental, just make sure you factor in the additional costs of their service into your plans and take an active role in selecting tenants. Ultimately, the person most interested in your success is you.

Property management may be able to help determine a proper rent. You can also use the online source Rentometer.com. Price your home at or below the median rent for the area.

If you plan on finding a renter yourself, you will need to obtain a rental agreement. This can be found online, at the local office supply store, or through a real estate attorney.

Begin advertising your home by placing a sign in the front yard and placing signs near the major streets near your home. You may also place ads in the newspaper or free online classifieds.

You will be taking all of the phone calls and showing the property to potential renters. Once you have a qualified applicant, simply run them through an online tenant background check. If they pass your minimum criteria, place them in your property.

You will collect a security deposit to help cover any damage that could be caused to your property. With proper screening, this will not be a huge worry.

There are many great resources on learning how to rent your house, finding the perfect tenants, and avoiding any legal issues in the process. Begin by searching your local library for material on this subject.

If your situation allows, you could rent a single room to a roommate. The roommate still signs a rental agreement holding them responsible for payments and damage caused. They would live out of one room in your house, but would have access to all 'public' locations within, such as the bathrooms, kitchen, and living room. This is an excellent way to reduce the amount of payment you are responsible for each month, but it comes with the sacrifice of less privacy and freedom inside your home.

An alternative to the roommate situation is to convert a shop, garage, or basement into a studio and rent it out.

If you are underwater in your mortgage, meaning you owe more than the house is worth or are behind on payments, you could consider selling to a professional real estate investor.

Real estate investors typically advertise on large billboards or small signs seen at street corners that read "We Buy Houses."

Call the number on the sign and let them know you need to sell your house, today. If the investor is interested in your property, they will discuss options with you. Investors may be interested in purchasing your house cash or they may want to take over payments and responsibility.

Many investors utilize a "Subject To" deal where they buy your house subject to the existing financing. You benefit by getting out from your mortgage payment without losing any money and are free from the property. The investor benefits by picking up a property that can be turned into cash flow if properly done. The risk is that the bank has the option to call the loan due since there was a transfer in ownership. Savvy investors have legal ways around any problems that may occur and have been successful at avoiding this.

If you are considering an investor, just make sure you go with someone you like and trust. Trust your gut instinct whether to move forward with the deal or not. It is rarely wrong.

Summary

This program only touches on the possibilities of reducing spending and debt. Your potential is endless and your limits are only set by your imagination.

After you reduce your spending and debt, begin implementing your strategies and continue to keep an eye out for a better deal. There may be a new option available where you can save even more. I moved one of my auto loans from the initial 8% interest to a new loan at only 3%. When I reached the final 6 month mark to accomplishing my goal, I transferred the loan once again to a credit card with a 0% introductory rate on cash advances.

I changed home and auto insurance companies multiple times throughout the years as I was paying off debt, because a more attractive offer presented itself. I would have never known of these deals if I had not kept my eyes open to the idea.

Write down your new debt-reduction goals on your "Financial Goals and Plan" worksheet and update your "Financial Balance" worksheet.

Congratulations on making additional progress toward your goals. You will reach your final goal in no time.

Determine Your Plan

How to Create Realistic, Obtainable Plans

Your plans must be realistic and obtainable to have any chance of success. The obtainment of goals builds your self confidence and helps to develop a successful mindset. When it comes to your final goal, only your imagination can set limitations. Without mental limitations, anything can be realistic and obtainable.

The best way to determine if your plan will work is to run it through the "Mental Scenario". Work your plan out in your head, or on paper, and actually calculate its development.

Pay attention to the date money comes in and when it gets applied towards debt. Do not forget to account for interest that will be charged to the outstanding balance each month. Also, don't forget to add some cushion space for unexpected bills or other expenses. Depending on your risk tolerance and your resources available, you will want to build some reserve into your plans.

Having an emergency cash fund is an option. Most financial advisors want you to have at least three month's salary in an emergency fund before you start paying off debt. This is never a bad idea, but personally,

I would rather see my money work for me instead of sitting in an account.

My alternative to the emergency cash fund was an open credit card. The card had a fixed interest rate for purchases and cash advances, and did not have annual fees. I didn't have to save money to achieve this emergency fund. I also did not pay interest as long as I the card went unused. I was able to have more than three months of my pay available at all times without having to work for it.

My wife and I were fortunate enough that we did not have to dip into our emergency fund for any reason. When we had unexpected expenses, we were able to use our "Debt Pay-Down Money" balance for funding. This set us back on our goals temporarily, but we benefit by making progress in our goals prior to this setback. This left us in an even better financial situation where we did not have to rely on the emergency fund as much because we were able to build our "Debt Pay-Down Money" balance. Typically, we could make up for these minor setbacks fairly quickly by picking up extra shifts at work, finding items around the house to sell, or performing side work.

If you don't have the option to open a credit card and your "Debt Pay-Down Money" balance is not sufficient, you should have some cash saved for an emergency. Your risk tolerance and goals will help determine how much this is. One method is to begin paying down your debt, but allocate some of your "Debt Pay-Down Money" towards this emergency fund, until a sufficient balance is achieved.

As you run your plans through mental scenarios, anticipate any problems that may occur. Are there any birthdays or holidays coming up? Any weddings or baby showers you will be attending? Consider any unexpected expense that could come up. A popped tire could prevent you from getting to work and would need to be replaced immediately. How you would work through this situation?

Allow room in your plans for fluctuations in spending. It is nearly impossible to estimate exactly how much money will leave in these categories. Even with a solid budget in place, you may find that certain spending categories require more money than expected. Gas prices or food prices may have gone up. Your car or house may be in need of a repair. Life happens, and it is always good practice to prepare for it.

We developed a "Planning Tool" that may help organize your mental process as you develop plans. This resource takes you through a series of questions that should be answered when developing plans. The benefit of running through this exercise is that you may find problem areas in your plans that you never knew existed. This "Planning Tool" can be downloaded for free at SAHDLife.com/DebtForms.

Make Plans That Adapt to Life

Your plans should be detailed and specific, but flexible at the same time. The plans you develop will need to be able to adapt to the ever-changing environment of real life.

Your plans are flexible, but your goals are not. When a problem occurs, look to change your plan, not your goal, to achieve success. There are many roads you can take to achieve the same goal. Sometimes, what initially appears to be the fastest way is not the most practical.

When I respond on an emergency, I try to take the fastest route to the scene. The freeway may appear to be the quickest and most direct path, but if I am traveling during rush hour I will be slowed down even with my lights and siren running. A more practical, and faster route in the end, would be to take one of the many side streets.

Think of this analogy when determining your plans. When you find one route that isn't working, it's time to take a side street that will still get you to your goal.

Your goals help guide your plans. They show you the end result you are striving to achieve. In the development of your plans, you want to take the most practical approach to achieving your goal first. As you carry out your plans, you want to keep your options open for an alternative.

It is not realistic to anticipate every problem you may run into. This is not the goal here. The goal is form a single plan that is realistic and obtainable, to anticipate potential problems, and to have a general idea of how you will deal with these problems so you can still achieve success.

On the ambulance, I may have a patient who is in need of a certain medication. The most practical and efficient way to deliver medications is through the veins, or an IV line. If I cannot obtain IV access, I need to find a different route to administer the medication. The end result, or the goal, is that the medication gets administered. How it happens isn't necessarily important, as long as the goal gets accomplished in the end.

Know your main plan and keep your alternative plans in the back of your mind. Think of it like a tool box. Certain problems require certain tools to fix them. The more knowledge you acquire and experience you obtain, the more tools you will add to your toolbox. These added tools will make future problem solving much easier.

Understand that life will happen, regardless of how much preparation you take. Your plans will almost never run through perfectly. Anticipate the roadblocks and embrace the challenge. Preparing for the problems ahead of time will allow you to take action much faster when the situation arises.

Assessing Your Risk Tolerance

Taking risk is not for everybody. Additional risk can add more stress. Depending on your personality, you may be able to handle this added stress, or you may live a much happier life while paying off debt with a more conservative plan. You will be achieving your goal either way.

Take an assessment of your risk tolerance to determine which plans will be realistic for you to put into action. We will discuss the benefits of taking on additional risk in this lesson.

The methods used to pay off your debt are organized by their risk levels into two categories: conventional and unconventional strategies.

Conventional strategies are those you see most people putting into practice. Although, at Debt Rescue, our conventional strategies may be more aggressive than other programs, they are generally considered low risk, low reward.

Unconventional strategies are "outside the box" ideas that people either dismiss as "impossible" or "too risky." Your level of risk tolerance will play a major role in your abilities to take action on these strategies. This approach is high risk, high reward.

One unconventional strategy we discussed earlier included selling your car for a loss and purchasing a cheaper vehicle.

Most people look at the immediate impact, or the perceived negative situation that was created through selling the car (the $2000 lost initially), instead of focusing on the long term benefit (saving $19,500 over the next 3 years).

Your mindset, if properly developed, will focus on the positive in any situation instead of trying to find the problem. While it is important to perform a risk/benefit assessment, you want to avoid immediately dismissing strategies before giving them a shot. Success will come through the application of creative thinking. Think creatively allows you to spend more of your "Intellectual Currency" than your hard earned money. Determine the goal you want to accomplish and think "How can I make this work?"

You will want to balance the amount of conventional and unconventional strategies you utilize in your plans. Creating a safe plan with too many conventional strategies will make for a slow process when paying off your debt. Sometimes playing it too safe can cost you more in the end.

Creating aggressive plans with too many unconventional strategies could place you at high risk of failure, especially if you do not have sufficient cash reserves available. This places you at risk of losing large amounts of money and possibly becoming bankrupt. An overly aggressive strategy may become too difficult to actually carry out over the long run. Keeping budgets tight with no cushion room will cause your plans to fall apart quick.

Conventional strategies will provide safety and security to your plans while still allowing you to accomplish your goals. Unconventional strategies will speed up your results when used appropriately. In order to achieve your final goal, you need to be willing to take some risks. Find a proper balance that fits your personality and tolerance level when creating your plans.

Establishing Rewards

Life is only worth living when you have fun doing so. Establishing rewards is more than having a good time while you pay off your debt. It is also important to the development of your mindset and reduction of stress.

Rewards bring with it great emotions of joy and happiness. When these emotions are connected with the successful completion of financial goals, the subconscious begins to develop an association.

Changing your mindset to finding happiness in completing your financial goals will keep you motivated to continue making progress. You will be more determined to face the challenges ahead and confident that you will conquer them.

The rewards you earn throughout the program will help relieve stress that debt and implementing aggressive financial strategies can bring. After completing a major milestone in your plans, there is no better way to clear your mind than to take a vacation.

In order for the vacation to be relaxing, it must come after the goal has been accomplished. You should take your reward as soon as possible after completing the goal in order to give yourself the most benefit.

With the successful completion of a goal, you are finally able to take a break and clear your mind from the previous stresses. This is a great time to enjoy life, relax and clear your mind.

A reward does not have to cost a lot of money. There is a fine balance between rewarding yourself and creating additional stress and debt. If your reward costs too much in money or time, you will set yourself back in progress unnecessarily.

Use the "Wants List" you established earlier to choose possible rewards. As you plan your strategies for paying off debt, be sure and establish which rewards will be earned and when you will receive them. You may want to refer to this list of rewards to keep yourself motivated through the process.

Life is about having fun and spreading love and joy to those around you. Life is too short to go without experiencing it to the fullest. You do not want to wait until you are completely debt free before allowing yourself any enjoyment. Begin living life today! Go to the places you wish to see. Do the things you wish to accomplish. Spend time with the people who are important in your life. The time to experience life and find enjoyment is now!

Execute

Take Immediate Action

There will never be a perfect time to start taking action. There is no magic formula or strategy for finding the perfect time to start your plans. The best time is right now.

You will never be completely ready to take on this task, and sitting back waiting for everything in your life to align perfectly will cost you more in time and money.

There is no silver bullet. Getting out of debt takes hard work and commitment to your goals. Your persistence and enthusiasm will keep you making progress even during the roughest times. You must perform the hard work and make the necessary decisions to accomplish your goals.

You will experience every emotion while working your plans. You will feel anger and frustration when your plans fail to work out perfectly. You will feel the fear of stepping into the unknown and not knowing the next step. You will find the faith that your strategies will work as long as you put everything you have into its success. You will also feel joy and happiness of overcoming obstacles and conquering your goals.

Do not let fear get in your way of taking immediate action. Develop your mindset to believe that with every failure comes an equal or greater success. Each failure is a step along the path to achieving your goals. As you start working through your problems and overcoming obstacles, you will reinforce these beliefs.

People have a habit of stopping at the first sign of failure. It has been programmed into our subconscious that failure means the end of the road has been reached. People fear ridicule and embarrassment from trying and being unsuccessful, so they give up.

Many inventors failed hundreds, if not thousands of times before being successful once. Many millionaires have tried and failed multiple times before becoming successful. Most self-made millionaires have been bankrupt at least once on their journey to riches. Each tried, failed, learned a lesson, and tried again until success was reached.

With application of the principles taught in these lessons, you will begin to reinforce the positive thoughts and memories in your subconscious. Future success will come easier as your mind draws positive, successful memories from the unconscious mind. In time, fear will go away and you will be fully optimistic about your future, no matter what it is you set your mind to accomplish. Until you reach this point, you will need to force yourself out of your comfort zone and take your fear head on.

This is the leap of faith. The first step is always the hardest because you feel you are blindly stepping forward, not knowing exactly what you are heading into.

The moment you realize you can't lose, you will stop living in fear. You will begin living without limitations. Once you realize you can accomplish anything you put your mind to, you will wonder why you never set higher standards for yourself. The world is plentiful. There is more than enough food, water, and resources for everyone on this planet, and the billions more that will accompany us in the future.

You have the power to create your life and the world around you. Believe in yourself and live without limitations. A whole new world will open up to you.

Lessons Learned

This final lesson serves the purpose of sharing problem areas I have experienced. It should serve as a lesson learned so the same mistake can be avoided as you develop your plans.

Not every conceivable issue could possibly be covered in this program. This lesson will go over a few unique situations I found important.

Overdraft Protection

On receiving a credit card from my bank, I was talked into setting it up as overdraft protection on my checking account. The idea was that I could avoid insufficient funds charges if my checking account were to overdraft and the purchase would instead go onto my credit card.

This sounded like a good idea. But, I should have looked into the details further. I knew my purchases would be charged 6% interest and I really did not plan on using the card very often. I planned on paying the minimum payment on the card each month because, at the time, the outstanding balance and interest charges did not bother me. I was more interested in spending the money I earned on fun things that I could enjoy now and was not focused on getting out of debt.

Fast forwarding into the future, the credit card balance was over $11,000 and I was making plans for getting out of debt. One day, I looked at the billing statement closely and noticed there were three different interest rate categories I was being charged. The lowest of the three was my standard purchase which was 6%. The other two were for balance transfers and cash advances. Each time the card was used to cover an overdraft from the checking account, it was considered a cash advance. The rate for a cash advance on this particular card was 20%.

I had been making minimum payments on the card throughout its use and taking a look at previous statements I noticed the cash advance balance had never gone down.

I decided to get a hold of the bank. During a phone conversation, I was told the minimum payment applies toward the lowest interest rate first. In order to pay off the higher rates, I would have to apply a larger payment than the minimum and specify where I want it applied.

Pay careful attention to your statements and be aware of programs advertised to 'protect' the card user.

Fixed Interest Rate

A few months later, the same card I managed to charge over $11,000 was slowly being paid down while my focus remained on higher priority debts. The interest rate on the card was 6%. For years prior, I had maintained a low balance on the card. With a large flow of medical bills, funding our move back to Washington State, and living off one income for a couple months, we really racked up a large debt. Within months of our credit card reaching its high balance, we received a notification in the mail that the bank was increasing our fixed interest rate from 6% to 13%.

My heart sunk. I did not know what to do. I considered transferring the balance to a new credit card, but I was unable to find one without a 3% balance transfer fee and I did not want to pay $330 in additional fees. I felt that if I paid the fee to transfer the card, I would only be faced with another inevitable interest rate hike. The increase in APR was going to change my interest payment from $55 to $120 a month. This meant less than half of the money I had available to pay on this debt would be applied toward the principal balance. I felt like I was being robbed.

I eventually found I was able to close the account and keep the current interest rate locked in. I wrote a letter to the bank of my intent to close the account. My account was soon closed at the 6% rate. As my wife and I continued implementing our financial strategies, we began making massive payments on the credit card. When the balance reached $3000, I received a letter from the bank offering to open the account and keep the interest rate at 6%. I denied the offer. I was done playing their games. This time, I won.

When dealing with loans and credit cards from the banks, you need to be aware of these and similar tactics. Their goal is to keep you in debt because this is the way they make money. The strategies presented in this course will allow you to play the same game, but shift the odds in your favor.

Medical Bill Payment Plan

After my son was born, we had a rush of medical bills. Everyone who had some part in the delivery and care was asking for their money and they wanted it now.

Years prior, I received a credit card with a high credit limit. I remember telling the bank I would rather have a limit of $1000 so I didn't overspend. They told me that it would be better to have a higher available limit in case of an emergency such as an unexpected medical bill or vehicle breakdown. I agreed, but was unsure if I would have the self-control to maintain a small balance on the card. When our medical bills began piling up, the card is the first thing I thought of.

This happened to be a very costly mistake. I added thousands of dollars onto a card which charged interest. If I had looked into the repayment programs offered by the medical companies, I would have found out that most hospitals, clinics, and other facilities offer affordable payment plans and do not collect interest off the balance owed. Many will structure repayment plans based off what you tell them is affordable for you at the time.

When we had our second child, I was able to make a 0% interest, minimum monthly payment of $5 on one of my accounts. I always paid on time making the minimum payment each month, but it was not the first bill I paid off in my debt elimination strategy. I was able to successfully defer the bill so I could focus on repayment of higher priority debts.

Monthly Meetings

When it came to doing the bills in our house, it was mostly a one-person job. Goal setting and creating plans was always a team effort, but the actual crunching of numbers and daily work maintaining the plans usually fell on one of us.

In the beginning of our relationship, I was in charge of the finances. As we began working to get ourselves out of debt, it became clear that communication was going to be an important issue. Even though we had worked as a team to get to the point we were, we would run into areas of confusion or frustration along the way.

We decided to implement a monthly meeting. We organized all of our income, debt, and spending onto a one-page form. This easy to read format gave us a quick update on our financial situation and allowed us to view the progress on our goals.

I have included the "Monthly Meeting" form at SAHDLife.com/DebtForms.

A year into us paying off our debt, my wife took over the bills and found many ways to accelerate our progress. There were times that it felt we were making unbelievable improvement. At times, I was sure we were running out of money. We would take vacations that made me wonder if we were going to still accomplish our financial goals on time. Using the monthly money meeting, my stress was relieved when I could see a visual update on our progress.

It is important to maintain a clear line of communication as you work through your own plans to financial success. The monthly meeting form is an excellent way to ensure everyone is up to date on the progress.

Not Following My Own Advice

At times, it was easy to lose sight of what is important in life by focusing on your problems. As I said in the beginning, all of the material presented in this program has come from trial and error. It has come from our drive to achieve greatness and our own failures. To start, we had to dig ourselves out of the financial hole we had created.

It was not easy. It was not fun. We thought as soon as we solved our debt problem, life would get better. But, as we continued working toward our goals, we began realizing our problems were not going away anytime soon. We had to find a way to reduce stress and enjoy life now.

I never imagined we would be able to accomplish what we had. We were able to work part time, go on many vacations, and spend more time with our children while getting out of debt

We followed a very aggressive plan and did experience both success and failure. At times, things would be going perfectly. I increased my hours at work to accelerate our progress so we could achieve our goals sooner. Then, with one unexpected expense after another, my confidence and faith was shot.

I would let anger, frustration, and negativity take over as I focused on the problems we faced. I needed to re-focus my energy.

Luckily, I have an outstanding wife who kept me on track and would keep me focused on the positive things in life. She has the power and drive to accomplish anything she puts her mind to, and has been a major portion of our success, both financially and in life. She not only strives to place us in a better financial situation, but she also delivers love and happiness to everyone in her life. Together, we have accomplished so much!

No matter how strong you feel you are, there will be those moments of weakness when you need inspiration and motivation to continue on. My wife and I motivate each other to accomplish more than we would have ever thought imaginable!

Printed in Great Britain
by Amazon

81606836R00073